WRITING IN THE
# SENIOR
# CAPSTONE
THEORY & PRACTICE

*Lea Masiello and Tracy L. Skipper*

Cite as:

Masiello, L., & Skipper, T. L. (2013). *Writing in the senior capstone: Theory and practice.* Columbia, SC: University of South Carolina, National Resource Center for The First-Year Experience and Students in Transition

Published by
National Resource Center for The First-Year Experience® and Students in Transition
University of South Carolina
1728 College Street, Columbia, SC 29208
www.sc.edu/fye

Production Staff for the National Resource Center
Project Manager: Tracy L. Skipper, Assistant Director of Publications
Design and Production: Josh Tyler, Graphic Artist
External Reviewers: Karen Weathermon, Director of Learning Communities, Washington State University; James Uhlenkamp, Writing Center Director, Graceland University

---

**Library of Congress Cataloging-in-Publication Data**

Masiello, Lea.
 Writing in the senior capstone : theory and practice / Lea Masiello and Tracy L. Skipper.
    pages cm
 Includes bibliographical references and index.
 ISBN 978-1-889271-87-3
1. College seniors—United States. 2. English language—Rhetoric. 3. Report writing. I. Title.
 LA229.M348 2013
 378.1'98--dc23
                                                            2013015219

# About the Publisher

The National Resource Center for The First-Year Experience and Students in Transition was born out of the success of the University of South Carolina's much-honored University 101 course and a series of annual conferences focused on the freshman-year experience. The momentum created by the educators attending these early conferences paved the way for the development of the National Resource Center, which was established at the University of South Carolina in 1986. As the National Resource Center broadened its focus to include other significant student transitions in higher education, it underwent several name changes, adopting the National Resource Center for The First-Year Experience and Students in Transition in 1998.

Today, the Center collaborates with its institutional partner, University 101 Programs, in pursuit of its mission to advance and support efforts to improve student learning and transitions into and through higher education. We achieve this mission by providing opportunities for the exchange of practical and scholarly information as well as the discussion of trends and issues in our field through convening conferences and other professional development events, such as institutes, workshops, and online learning opportunities; publishing scholarly practice books, research reports, a peer-reviewed journal, electronic newsletters, and guides; generating, supporting, and disseminating research and scholarship; hosting visiting scholars; and maintaining several online channels for resource sharing and communication, including a dynamic website, listservs, and social media outlets.

The National Resource Center is the trusted expert, internationally recognized leader, and clearinghouse for scholarship, policy, and best practice for all postsecondary student transitions.

## Institutional Home

The National Resource Center is located at the University of South Carolina's flagship campus in Columbia. The mission of USC Columbia, founded in 1801, is twofold: to establish and maintain excellence in its student population, faculty, academic programs, living and learning environment, technological infrastructure, library resources, research and scholarship, and public and private support and endowment and to enhance the industrial, economic, and cultural potential of the state. The Columbia campus offers 324 degree programs through its 14 degree-granting colleges and schools. Students have been awarded more than $16.7 million for national scholarships and fellowships since 1994. In fiscal year 2012, faculty generated $238 million in funding for research, outreach, and training programs. Carolina is one of only 63 public universities listed by the Carnegie Foundation in the highest tier of research institutions in the United States.

# Contents

# Tables
## and Figures

# Preface

Culminating experiences for undergraduates may include theses, final projects, recitals, internships, capstone courses in the major, or seminars emphasizing professional preparation or the transition out of college. However they are configured, capstones are designed to help students synthesize learning experiences in a particular major or across the undergraduate curriculum. They share a common purpose of helping students integrate their learning by reflecting on their undergraduate academic, and in some cases, social experiences. As will be seen in chapter 1, writing assignments are common components of most capstone experiences. Therefore, this book explores two questions with respect to writing instruction in the senior seminar or capstone course.

First, to what extent is the current emphasis on writing helping students develop the communication and critical-thinking skills needed for a range of professional, personal, and civic pursuits following graduation? While developing communication and critical-thinking skills are important goals for many senior capstones, they are by no means the only ones, which leads to the second question. To what extent can writing facilitate the achievement of these other capstone goals? The first part of this book draws on the research and practice literature to answer these questions, suggesting that writing activities can meet general course goals in intellectual development, such as helping to improve skills in critical thinking, mastery of disciplinary content, and oral and written communication. Writing projects in the senior capstone also can promote personal attributes that employers seek (e.g., collaboration, independence, innovation). Finally, students can create writing projects to reflect on and showcase their learning in the major and across disciplines. These projects also may provide faculty and administrators with useful documents for departmental and programmatic assessments.

Yet, understanding the importance of writing in a course like the senior capstone is of little value if faculty do not have the confidence or skills to incorporate more writing and more effective writing assignments in their courses. To that end, the second part of this book focuses on strategies for maximizing the usefulness of writing in the senior capstone. Here, the authors draw on their combined experience teaching writing at the college level, knowledge of adult learning and development, and understanding of high-impact educational practices to describe strategies for using writing to help students meet a range of academic, personal, and professional goals in the senior capstone.

For example, Lea has more than 35 years of experience as an English faculty member at the college level. She has taught writing workshops in summer programs for underprepared students, first-year college writing, research writing, technical writing, public speaking, American literature, and an interdisciplinary senior seminar on The National Parks. In the senior seminar, in particular, she found students flourished with the opportunity to develop a project of their choosing; working in small groups to create both individual and group portfolios; researching one park in depth; and responding to critical economic, environmental, and cultural issues facing the park. Many students chose the option of connecting their individual research to their major. For example, a marketing major might design a promotional campaign to increase visitation to more remote parks. Or, a middle-grades education major might create a series of lesson plans on Yellowstone National Park for a social studies unit. These kinds of assignments were more than simply academic, as one former student reported that she found her dream job working for the Pennsylvania Department of Conservation and Natural Resources, a position that united her skills in technology and writing with her passion for protecting the natural world.

In addition to her years in the classroom, Lea has directed writing centers, coordinated writing programs, and served on university committees to develop writing curricula. All of these roles have helped her gain an understanding of the challenges and frustrations—especially with respect to workload—that faculty experience when they integrate writing into their course content.

Similarly, Tracy has 12 years of experience teaching writing at the college level and has conducted workshops for faculty and staff on the design and assessment of writing assignments and on strategies for developing their own writing skills. She also has researched the connection between students' cognitive development and their ability to write effective arguments. Beyond these areas, Tracy draws on research conducted by the National Resource Center for The First-Year Experience and Students in Transition on the senior capstone experience and other high-impact educational practices to inform our understanding of writing instruction outside the composition classroom.

The authors draw on this collective knowledge and experience, the work of colleagues across the country, and the research and practice literature to offer a range of strategies for assigning writing, helping students develop as writers and thinkers, and responding to student work within the context of the senior capstone.

## Principles and Assumptions

The senior capstone offers a rich context for enhancing oral and written communication skills, while challenging students to explore new ways of thinking, reflecting, and understanding ideas and information that truly matter to them. The first part of this book delineates the principles and assumptions emerging from theory and research that undergird the suggestions for practice in the second part of the book. These principles include the following key points:

- Establishing a theoretical foundation helps instructors create a stronger, clearer, and ultimately more coherent set of practices that will benefit student learning and increase the likelihood that instructors will achieve their curricular objectives.

- Students will learn more when instructors regard them as evolving people, with complex lives and situations that intersect with their development as writers.

- Students can become agents of change through writing experiences. They may become people committed to an ethical, responsible use of argument and persuasion for the good of their communities.

- A rhetorical approach to writing assignments, instruction, response, and assessment helps reinforce learning by creating congruence in critical-thinking tasks (e.g., analysis, synthesis, evaluation) applicable to both written and oral communication contexts.

- Students can improve as writers and speakers through practice, given adequate time to develop and change.

- Writers need to be interdependent communicators, with the ability to work autonomously, creatively, and clearly. They also need to be comfortable working collaboratively, cooperating with peers and other individuals who are part of their social contexts, to meet the needs of their audience.

- Writing activities (e.g., all elements of drafting and revising, conferencing, and self-assessment) can facilitate students' personal and intellectual development.

- By working with a variety of genres that include workplace writing as well as traditional academic formats, students expand their repertoire of writing strategies, tools, techniques, and skills, helping them succeed in the community, workplace, or graduate school.

- By articulating their strengths and weaknesses as writers and thinkers, students can create bridges to new knowledge and understanding, facilitating the transfer of learning.

## Overview

Part I of the book has a three-fold agenda: (a) to help readers understand the role writing currently plays in the senior capstone, (b) to suggest important connections between learning and development goals and writing instruction, and (c) to provide general guidelines for how and why to build more writing into the course. Writing appears to be a fixture within the culminating experience. As such, some readers may question the need for such a justification for writing within the capstone course. However, the information contained here might provide a useful framework for training workshops for faculty new to teaching in the senior capstone or for ongoing faculty development efforts. At institutions where capstone experiences are being introduced for the first time or undergoing major reconfiguration, this discussion might offer guidance for shaping those experiences.

In chapter 1, the authors rely on national data and published accounts of senior seminars to define the course, describe its goals, and identify the role writing currently plays in such courses. How focusing on writing in the senior capstone can help institutions respond to the expectations for specific learning outcomes from employers, graduate schools, and other entities is also considered.

Chapter 2 begins by exploring the connection between common goals of the senior capstone and the developmental tasks students face near the end of their undergraduate experience. We identify a range of assignments currently used in seminars and describe how these assignments support students' personal and intellectual development. The chapter closes by suggesting other types of assignments that might be included to further facilitate student learning and development.

The final chapter of part I draws on the National Council of Teachers of English's (NCTE, 2004) *Beliefs About the Teaching of Writing* to create a rough outline for the incorporation of writing within the capstone course. The chapter explores the connections among writing, speaking, and thinking; describes strategies for supporting the development of writing across a wide range of genres; and offers suggestions on responding to student writing.

Part II fills in the rough outline introduced in chapter 3 by providing more detailed strategies for incorporating specific types of writing in the senior capstone. Here, readers will find practical suggestions for (a) incorporating informal writing in the seminar to develop communication, critical-thinking, and research skills; (b) embedding portfolios to facilitate student learning and program assessment;

(c) supporting the development of a capstone research project; and (d) using writing to facilitate the development of oral communication. While some of the activities and assignments may be new to many senior capstones, they can support the development of end products typically associated with the course, such as independent research projects, essays synthesizing disciplinary (or interdisciplinary) perspectives on an issue, or policy papers. Thus, rather than being added burdens to the student or instructor, many of the suggestions included here are designed to facilitate successful completion of assignments already in place in many courses.

In chapter 4, instructors find ideas for using informal and unrevised writing to help students develop more formal written products, explore their own understanding of a topic, synthesize information, and/or work out provisional solutions to problems. In particular, two strategies—freewriting and journaling—are examined for their potential to support student learning and development.

Chapter 5 offers ideas for designing portfolio assignments as end-products for the senior capstone that help students demonstrate a range of skills, while reflecting on their learning experiences. The portfolio both facilitates student learning and development and is a potent evaluation tool for the seminar, the major, or possibly the entire undergraduate experience.

At many institutions, the culminating experience is an independent research project, yet many students will have had limited exposure to research design and processes before the senior year. Chapter 6 provides strategies for helping students define a compelling research question, analyze the literature, and document the research process. In particular, readers are introduced to the research portfolio—a collection of research critiques, workplace documents, web-based assignments, and other genres—that builds students' understanding of the research process while providing them with an opportunity to develop valuable academic and workplace writing skills.

There are good reasons for asking students to work on more extensive research and writing projects, and the research essay, for example, can contribute to students' personal, professional, and intellectual growth. In particular, it can help students develop an understanding and mastery of the skills needed to make successful arguments in academic, professional, and civic conversations. Chapter 7 explores the skills from the classical rhetorical tradition and modern academic conventions that students need to create an effective final project.

In addition to writing ability, employers also seek graduates with strong oral communication skills. The final chapter examines the links between writing and speaking, in particular, the ways in which writing assignments support the development of strong academic presentations and, conversely, how oral communication facilitates writing. An oral communication component in the senior capstone will help students develop confidence, authority, and identity as members of their disciplinary and professional communities. This chapter offers strategies for helping students achieve these outcomes. The book concludes by pulling together strategies and recommendations found throughout for successful inclusion of writing assignments in the senior capstone.

Teaching is a joy and privilege, and nurturing writers takes patience and a caring commitment to intellectual excellence. We hope that the information, ideas, and suggestions in this book will make instructors more comfortable and confident incorporating writing activities into the senior capstone. Moreover, we see writing instruction in a capstone course as a valuable instrument for helping students achieve their personal, professional, and academic goals and for helping colleges and universities demonstrate the effectiveness of particular programs of study and of undergraduate education more broadly.

# Part I

Foundations for Writing
in the Senior Capstone

# Chapter 1

## The Senior Capstone and Writing Instruction: Helping Students Look Back and Move Forward

Although the culminating or capstone experience for undergraduate education began much earlier, it gained prominence in the late 1980s and early 1990s, largely in response to national calls for education reform. In particular, many campuses[1] pointed to the increasing fragmentation and specialization of the undergraduate curriculum, citing the 1985 report from the Association of American Colleges (AAC, now the Association of American Colleges and Universities, AAC&U), *Integrity in the College Curriculum: A Report to the Academic Community*. Essentially, this report argued that as a loose collection of courses tacked on to two years of more general coursework, the major lacked coherence for most students. In addition to educational experiences that helped students gain literacy and inquiry skills, among others, the AAC report called for an enriched major based on

> a central core of method or theory [with] a structure that forces students to experience the range of topics addressed by the discipline, a sequence that assumes advancing sophistication, and a final project or thesis that provides the student with a means to demonstrate mastery of the area's complexity. (Troyer, 1993, p. 246)

Today, the capstone experience can take many forms—a disciplinary or interdisciplinary seminar, a senior thesis, a gallery show or recital, or portfolio—although a 2011 national survey (Padgett & Kilgo, 2012) suggested the disciplinary seminar is the most common. This chapter briefly defines the senior seminar

---

[1]A search of the literature revealed more than 40 conference presentations and published articles describing senior capstone courses or seminars from 1979 through 2011. Presentations and articles published in the early 1990s frequently referenced calls for educational reforms as the impetus for the creation or revision of the senior seminar.

and capstone course and describes their prevalence in American higher education. Descriptions of capstone courses drawn from the literature and national data are used to highlight important goals, in particular the development of writing skills. Finally, a rationale is offered for why a culminating experience with a strong emphasis on the development of written and oral communication skills is essential in the undergraduate curriculum.

## Definition and Prevalence of Senior Seminars and Capstone Courses

The senior seminar frequently is defined as a synthesizing experience, one "with the specific objective of integrating a body of relatively fragmented knowledge into a unified whole" (Durel, 1993, p. 223) and of "requir[ing] students to apply what they have already learned" (Seeborg, 2008, p. 63). Troyer (1993) noted the integrative focus is typically conceived in two different ways. The first emphasizes integration across the undergraduate curriculum. While students might focus on special projects within the major as a culminating experience, they are encouraged to reflect on and think critically about the intersections with other disciplines and the ways in which other methodological and theoretical frameworks might inform explorations of questions in their own discipline. The second, and more common, approach focuses on synthesis of disciplinary content to master a particular subject matter.

Others point to the senior seminar as "a rite of passage that marks the abandonment of one status and the assumption of another" (Hauhart & Grahe, 2010, p. 4). As with the concept of integration, the rite of passage is typically conceived in one of two ways. For some, this passage is defined rather narrowly, as entry into a particular disciplinary community (Fleron & Hotchkiss, 2001; McElroy, 1997). Here, the goal is to help individuals move from the role of students to full-fledged community members who think and speak the language of economics, mathematics, engineering, sociology, and so on. Others frame the notion of rite of passage more broadly, as a foundation for lifelong learning. For example, Durel (1993) noted, "this course provides an experience through which undergraduate students both look back over their undergraduate curriculum in an effort to make sense of that experience and look forward to a life by building on that experience" (p. 223).

Henscheid (2000) reported that formal efforts to document the prevalence of senior seminars date back to the 1970s. In 1998, the National Resource Center for The First-Year Experience and Students in Transition conducted a national survey of senior seminars and capstone courses. Slightly more than three quarters of institutions responding offered a senior seminar. Recent surveys suggest the presence of these courses may be increasing. In a national survey conducted by the John N. Gardner Institute for Excellence in Undergraduate Education, 93.1% of respondents indicated they offered a seminar for seniors (Barefoot, Griffin, & Koch, 2012). This is consistent with findings from a 2011 national study of capstone experiences in which 97.1% of respondents reported offering one or more culminating experiences for seniors (Padgett & Kilgo, 2012).

National survey data and a review of published course descriptions provide some insight into how senior seminars are organized. Most courses appear to be discipline based. For example, Padgett and Kilgo (2012) reported that 84.7% of institutions responding to a survey of senior capstone experiences offered a discipline-based course, the primary type of capstone experience on nearly 60% of campuses. One third (33.2%) had an interdisciplinary course, representing a primary type of experience on fewer than 13% of campuses. These percentages are consistent with earlier findings reported by Henscheid (2000) in which the majority of courses offered were discipline based (70.3%) compared to interdisciplinary (16.3%).

Published course descriptions suggest variance in the way individual courses are organized, although two models seem to dominate. In the first model, the senior seminar functions as an adjunct course, offering support and structure for students completing an independent project. The class may meet weekly for the first few weeks of the academic term to introduce the research project and provide students an orientation to research methods of the discipline. Once students have developed a proposal for their individual projects, formal class meetings become less frequent. Instead, students often participate in individual conferences with the seminar instructor or with an affiliated faculty member directing the project. Limited class meetings may give students an opportunity to report on their progress, respond to drafts of peers' work, or present their projects to their classmates. Findings from a national survey of capstone experiences (Padgett & Kilgo, 2012) confirmed the prevalence of this model. Project-based capstone experiences were the second most common type of experience reported, occurring at 64.6% of responding institutions. On those campuses where project-based experiences were the primary culminating experience for seniors, nearly two thirds (62.7%) indicated it included an instructor-led class.

A second theme emerging from published descriptions of senior seminars underscores the integrative purpose at the heart of many of these courses. In this type of seminar, students prepare presentations on selected topics or readings designed to synthesize disciplinary knowledge and/or apply it to current issues or problems. While students may still be required to produce a major essay or research project, the individual projects seem to play a less central role in the structure of the course. For example, the English capstone course at Indiana University of Pennsylvania (IUP), part of a curriculum revision of the major, serves as the bookend to the first-year introductory seminar (W. Carse, personal communication, August 28, 2012). In this capstone course, English majors from all departmental tracks (i.e., film; language; writing; or textual, cultural, and literary studies) gather to share their expertise and are mentored for professional development, including preparing applications for graduate school or employment. Basic course objectives include applying and integrating theories and methods from the students' chosen areas of concentration (e.g., linguistics and rhetoric or literary and cultural theories) and analyzing texts (i.e., literary, film, cultural, and language) to answer the question, How are theories of knowledge in the field of English constructed? (W. Carse, personal communication, August 28, 2012). Students create portfolios, which include a final project. They are encouraged to present their research or creative works at the yearly English Undergraduate Conference.

Writing plays a major role in many senior seminars, no matter how they are organized. Additional details about the types of writing assignments present in these courses will be described below.

## Goals of Senior Capstones

Given the definition of senior seminars above, it is perhaps not surprising that integration is central to many courses. Henscheid (2000) reported that fostering integration and synthesis within the academic major was the most frequently reported goal among respondents to a national survey of senior seminars. Other important goals for these courses focused on the transition from college to career—promoting integration and connections between the academic major and work world and improving seniors' career preparation and preprofessional development. More recently, Padgett and Kilgo (2012) found that the five most commonly cited objectives for senior courses or capstones were

- critical-thinking and/or analytic or problem-solving skills (49.6%),
- ability to conduct scholarly research (27.6%),
- career preparation (25.0%),
- professional development (23.5%), and
- proficiency in written communication (22.8%).

It is important to note that the 2011 National Survey of Senior Capstone Experiences did not list integration and/or synthesis as response options, so their absence should not be interpreted as a change in focus for the course. Rather, evidence from this survey suggests an ongoing emphasis on these processes. Slightly more than 10% of the respondents provided some other objective for the course (Padgett & Kilgo, 2012). Of those other objectives, approximately 40% mentioned integration and/or synthesis within the major or across the under-graduate experience. Similarly, respondents were asked to identify practices that were incorporated into the senior experience. Of those responding, 60.1% indicated that the senior capstone included integrative learning (i.e., between courses or between coursework and life)—the most frequently reported practice.

Padgett and Kilgo's (2012) findings mirrored those of a national survey of student success and retention initiatives. Barefoot and her colleagues (2012) reported (a) demonstration of major-related competencies, 90%; (b) creation or presentation of original research or artistic expression, 78%; and (c) career readiness, 57%, as important goals for the senior seminar. A review of published descriptions of senior seminars provided greater insight into how goals are defined at the course level and suggested some goals not fully captured by national surveys. For example, a common goal of senior seminars is to bring coherence to an academic discipline, but more specifically, these courses seek to help students appreciate the discipline. In this way, they seem to function as an ongoing recruitment effort for majors, helping students solidify their commitment and investment to the field.[2] Such efforts vary by discipline as can be seen in the nature of the projects students undertake in the senior seminar. For example, Fleron and Hotchkiss (2001) noted the senior seminar in mathematics at Westfield State College is designed "to illustrate how the courses our students have taken as part of their degree program provide the necessary tools, habits of mind, and background for playing an active role in the ongoing development of the field of mathematics" (p. 292). Similarly, a senior seminar at Virginia Tech "introduce[s] undergraduates to the researching, writing, and publishing experiences of working

---

[2] Tinto's (1993) model of student departure provides some insight into this idea of ongoing recruitment for the major. Once students make an initial commitment to an institution (or a major), their academic and social experiences—both formal and informal—provide a framework for confirming or revising those initial commitments. If students do not find membership within their disciplinary community or find that they are out of sync with the values and norms of that community, they may question their major and/or career decisions. To the extent that the seminar helps students find areas of alignment between the discipline and their personal values and goals, they are able to affirm their earlier choices.

historians" (Stephens, Jones, & Barrow, 2011, p. 65). In both cases, the projects result in traditional academic products (e.g., mathematical proofs, historical essays drawing on the analysis of primary documents), suggesting that the ongoing connection to the discipline is primarily academic (i.e., pursuing graduate education and teaching at the college level).

In other courses, the desired connection to the major has a more professional focus (i.e., applying disciplinary knowledge to work in corporate, government, or nonprofit settings). For example, Ellings, Rush, and Cushman (1989) described a seminar at the University of Washington that aimed to provide students with the opportunity to deal with public policy questions in a real-world setting. That is, the work of the course mirrored what students could expect in government or corporate jobs following graduation. The goals of a writing-intensive capstone in electrical and computer engineering at the University of Arizona similarly suggested preparation for entry into a profession other than academe. Students were expected to produce a range of documents that they might develop in a work setting, such as a project proposal, a memorandum taking a clear position, and technical reports for both engineering and nonengineering audiences (Ostheimer & White, 2005).

Schmid (1993) identified articulating the relationship between the discipline and students' current and future lives as one of the core challenges and "central objective[s]" of the senior seminar (p. 220). He noted that, while students in his department indicated their sociology major was related to future vocational choices (e.g., human services, corrections, human relations), they were unable to articulate those connections. An emphasis on traditional academic projects rather than workplace documents is unlikely to illuminate those connections for students. Troyer (1993) found fewer than 5% of students in the sociology department at Drake University went on to graduate school in that field. In this respect, senior seminars that use the "materials of the discipline … to address broader questions and issues required for citizens of a global community" (Troyer, p. 247) ultimately may be more successful in cultivating an ongoing connection to the major and related career fields.

## The Role of Writing in the Senior Capstone

The descriptions of senior seminars and capstones available in the literature suggest that writing plays a prominent role in these courses and that the types of assignments present are varied. Further, the assignments support prominent goals of capstone courses. Table 1.1 provides an overview of writing assignments found in a review of some 40 course descriptions published between 1979 and 2011.

Table 1.1
*Writing Assignments in Senior Capstones*

| Type of Assignment | Times Reported |
| --- | --- |
| Traditional academic research paper | 13 |
| Report of original research | 11 |
| Short, expository essays | 8 |
| Written responses to assigned readings | 6 |
| Peer review | 6 |
| Personal or reflective writing | 5 |
| Applied writing assignments | 4 |
| Career-related writing products | 3 |
| Informal writing assignments | 2 |
| Revision of an existing paper | 2 |
| Essay exam | 2 |

While many seminars engage students in the design and completion of an original research project grounded in the methodology of their discipline, the library research paper is still common. Whatever the form, these longer written projects frequently make use of best practices in writing pedagogy—encouraging students to write multiple drafts of the paper and providing opportunities for peer and/or instructor review of early drafts. In some cases, these projects are conceived of as staged writing assignments. In an economics capstone at St. Mary's College, for example, students were challenged to "produce a scholarly article worthy of consideration for conference presentation or journal submission" (McElroy, 1997, p. 32). For this assignment, students produced five mini drafts over the semester, including a proposal, a literature review, and methodology and results sections. A fourth draft combined the first three mini drafts and added a conclusion. The final version was a fully revised draft that included references and an abstract. Such large-scale projects, especially when focused on independent research, can support seminar goals related to critical thinking, problem solving, and scholarly research.

Senior capstones incorporate a variety of other types of writing, which also support the larger goals of the course. For example, many seminars require students to write short expository essays or to produce formal or informal responses to the course readings or activities. These responses are variously framed as summaries (Wallner & Latosi-Sawin, 1999), critiques (Cardillo & Koritz, 1979; Seeborg, 2008), or analyses (Ervin, 1998; Fleron & Hotchkiss, 2001; Troyer, 1993). To the extent that the responses veer toward critique and analysis, they help students hone their critical-thinking skills and encourage them to enter into the professional conversation of the discipline or field. In some cases, these responses allow students to synthesize course readings as relates to their own learning or the larger disciplinary conversation (Fleron & Hotchkiss, 2001; Zechmeister & Reich, 1994). Reflective-writing assignments—such as an intellectual autobiography (Smith, 1993; Troyer, 1993)—may also engage students in analysis and synthesis. In this way, many of the writing assignments in the capstone underscore and support the integrative function of the course in the undergraduate curriculum.

Writing assignments in the senior capstone also support students' career development and preparation for entry into the world of work. Though reported less frequently, some courses ask students to produce résumés or cover letters (Hathaway & Atkinson, 2001; Wallner & Latosi-Sawin, 1999) and to research and write short reports on the job outlook for their field (Hathaway & Atkinson, 2001; Zechmeister & Reich, 1994). To the extent that senior capstones move away from traditional academic writing assignments toward more applied writing projects, they support the students' professional development. In some courses, seniors were engaged in writing grant proposals (Ervin, 1998; Worthy, Taylor, & Cheek, 2008), speeches and press releases (Ervin, 1998), memoranda (Ostheimer & White, 2005), and technical reports (Ostheimer & White, 2005; Wei, Siow, & Burley, 2007). Similarly, opportunities for peer review in the capstone may help students gain facility in the more collaborative writing process that frequently occurs in professional settings.

## A Renewed Interest in the Senior Capstone

The earlier review of national survey data in this chapter seems to suggest that senior seminars remain a prominent feature of the undergraduate curriculum and may, in fact, be on the rise. This continued—or, in some cases, renewed—interest can no doubt be linked to two interconnected concerns related to American higher education at this time. The first is a desire to ensure that students have achieved the hallmarks of a college-educated person in the 21st century. Closely related are pressures for students to possess the skills and attributes leading to stable employment as they enter the workforce. The final section of this chapter examines these dual concerns and highlights the role of the senior capstone and the writing embedded within it in helping higher education achieve its aims.

### *Acquisition of 21st Century Learning Outcomes*

*College Learning for the New Global Century*, a Liberal Education and America's Promise (LEAP) initiative report (AAC&U, 2007), identified four essential learning outcomes for college graduates entering the global workforce: (a) knowledge of human cultures and the physical and natural world, (b) intellectual and practical skills, (c) personal and social responsibility, and (d) integrative and applied learning. An earlier report (Leskes & Miller, 2006) framed these outcomes in slightly different terms, labeling them integrative learning, inquiry learning, global learning, and civic learning. Inquiry learning, closely related to intellectual and practical skills, is

> a process in which learners seek their own theories, answers, or solutions; conduct investigations, building methodological skills in systematic ways; gather knowledge as it is needed to pursue lines of questioning typical of experienced practitioners; [and] ask questions and investigate issues in ways characteristic of disciplines, thereby learning to think like experts in that field. (Leskes & Miller, 2006, p. 19)

Integrative learning involves drawing on "diverse points of view; understand[ing] issues contextually; connect[ing] knowledge and skills from multiple sources and experiences; [and] adapt[ing] learning from one situation to another, applying it in varied settings" (Leskes & Miller, 2006, p. 17). While bringing multiple disciplinary perspectives to bear on contemporary issues is one path to integrative learning, linking theory to practice also can facilitate this outcome for students (Leskes & Miller, 2006). Applied- and experiential-learning opportunities (e.g., service-learning, internships, undergraduate research) are key sites for integrative learning.

Schneider (2008) identified a number of common educational practices that show particular promise in helping students achieve 21st century learning outcomes. These practices included common intellectual experiences, undergraduate research, thematic learning communities, first-year seminars, capstone courses, writing- or skills-intensive courses, internships, collaborative learning experiences, and service or community-based learning. In examining their characteristics, Kuh (2008) labeled such activities *high-impact practices* (HIPs) because they have been routinely linked to "increase[d] rates of student retention and engagement" (p. 9). He argued their effectiveness stems from a number of key factors. First, HIPs demand not only that students devote considerable time but also significant effort in completing educationally purposeful tasks. These activities also engage students with faculty and their peers in formal and informal conversations "about substantive matters, typically over an extended period of time" (Kuh, p. 14). HIPs frequently engage students in authentic learning tasks, meaning they have the opportunity to apply knowledge gained in the classroom to problems and situations on the campus and in the community. The interaction with peers and faculty and opportunities for real-world learning experiences also increase the likelihood that students will encounter people who are different from themselves. Such experiences "challenge students to develop new ways of thinking about and responding immediately to novel circumstances" (Kuh, p. 15). Finally, HIPs are effective in helping students achieve important learning outcomes because individuals participating in these activities typically receive frequent feedback about their performance, which allows them to make adjustments and increases the likelihood of their achieving outcomes in the future.

As a high-impact activity, capstone projects and culminating experiences have been identified as helping students achieve outcomes related to knowledge of human cultures and the physical and natural world and integrative and applied learning (Schneider, 2008). To the extent that capstone experiences involve independent research supervised by a faculty mentor, such experiences also support a range of intellectual and practical skills, including inquiry and analysis, critical and creative thinking, and written and oral communication. In short, senior capstones appear well positioned to help students achieve outcomes related to both integrative and inquiry learning.

### Preparation for the Transition Out of College

On the one hand, capstone courses seek to ensure that students graduate having achieved a baseline competence in universally important learning outcomes. On the other, these courses also are designed to ensure that students have the knowledge, skills, and dispositions needed once they transition out of college—whether that is immediately into the world of work or into graduate or professional education. The skills demanded by employers and graduate educators dovetail in important ways with the learning outcomes identified above. In particular, the development of written and oral communication—both as a facilitator for intellectual skill development and as a practical skill in itself—is critical for postcollege success.

A 2006 survey sponsored by the LEAP initiative (AAC&U, 2007) asked employers upon which learning outcomes colleges should place more emphasis. Among intellectual and practical skills, the three most commonly identified outcomes included (a) teamwork skills in diverse groups, 76%; (b) critical thinking and analytic reasoning, 73%; and (c) written and oral communication, 73%. In terms of integrative learning, 73% of employers responded that colleges should emphasize the application of knowledge in real-world settings. A more recent report (Hart Research Associates, 2010) suggested employers' expectations have increased since the 2008 recession. In this survey, the three areas most commonly noted as needing more attention in the undergraduate curriculum related to oral and written communication (89%), critical and analytical thinking (81%), and application of knowledge and skills to real-world settings (79%).

Similar to these findings, the *Job Outlook* from the National Association of Colleges and Employers (NACE, 2009) identified written and oral communication skills at the very top of desirable attributes for employees but also suggested that students are not receiving adequate preparation in this area. This conclusion is consistent with earlier research. For example, in 2006, The Conference Board (with Corporate Voices for Working Families, the Partnership for 21st Century Skills, and the Society for Human Resource Management) surveyed more than 400 employers regarding graduates' readiness for the workforce. These respondents ranked oral and written communication skills in the very top tier of the most important competencies graduates need for success, yet they also noted that new employees from every sector—high school and two- and four-year colleges—were deficient in these areas, along with critical thinking and problem-solving abilities. When asked which educational practices would be most useful in helping students prepare for the workforce, 84% of employers agreed that a senior project requiring students to demonstrate depth of knowledge in their fields along with analytic, problem-solving, and communication skills was a valuable experience (Hart Research Associates, 2010). In other words, employers see the current focus on project-based writing assignments in many senior capstones as a useful career development and/or preparation experience.

### The Transition Into Graduate Study

Employers are important stakeholders in college outcomes as are graduate and professional schools. Graduate faculty expect to see competence in analysis and synthesis and originality in written expression. More philosophically, they want to see evidence of the inquiring mind as well as independence in discovering topics for research and study (Fischer & Zigmond, 1998). Mullen (2006) identified specific attributes graduate students need, including high-level reading comprehension and advanced critical skills that would allow them to analyze rhetorical structures, create an audience-driven document, participate in writing workshops and collaborative processes, and write for specific professional and academic genres. Graduate students need to be able to handle a range of written documents independently, such as progress reports on research projects, publications in scholarly journals, job application letters and dossiers that may be included in a portfolio, and grant applications. While the senior research project builds competence in some of these genres, Mullen suggested several additional writing activities designed to support development in other areas (e.g., research journals that reflect on interviews and record observations while working out data interpretation, reviews of articles or books that tie into a research project). In short, as with immediate transition into the workforce, success in graduate school appears to be mediated by facility in oral and written communication.

## Conclusion

A 1998 report from the Boyer Commission identified effective communication skills as essential for new graduates and singled out a capstone project incorporating collaboration, teamwork, inquiry, analysis, problem solving, and opportunities for oral and written expression, as an ideal vehicle for helping students achieve these aims. However, a 2001 follow-up to this report (Boyer Commission) noted that, while the development of writing skills may be strong in first-year courses, it was not adequately promoted at the advanced and professional level.

Recognizing this disconnect and hoping to increase intellectual challenge at UCLA, the vice provost for undergraduate education took the bold step of encouraging all departments to develop capstone projects, defining the form of the projects to fit the methodological training of their discipline (Berrett, 2012). The projects included original laboratory research in sciences, theses in advanced seminars in the humanities and music history, and scholarly publications from fieldwork in marine biology and ecology, behavior, and evolution.

Innovative business labs were led by teaching assistants and integrated alumni, who critiqued students' presentations and helped them understand the intellectual demands of employment (Berrett, 2012). Responding to concerns that students could not handle the difficulty of such capstone projects, especially projects that involved writing, the vice provost asked, "If the students aren't capable of doing some kind of paper, what kind of education are you giving them?" (Berrett, 2012, p. A11).

Despite efforts such as these, a gap between students' writing in their majors and writing for their professional lives persists at many institutions. This chapter has argued that writing activities hold tremendous potential value for college graduates as they move into the workforce or advanced educational settings. Future chapters will offer strategies for refining the senior project and for incorporating a wider range of writing activities into the senior capstone that can promote both the goals of the individual course and the broader aims of undergraduate education.

# Chapter 2

## The Role of Writing in the Capstone: Supporting Personal and Intellectual Development

As previously noted, goals for senior capstones frequently include those related to the development of critical- and analytic-reasoning skills, career readiness, and communication skills. Despite a focus on these types of outcomes, Henscheid (2008) reported that many employers "give college graduates low scores for their preparedness in global knowledge, self-direction, writing, critical thinking, and adaptability" (p. 20). While many of these abilities can be addressed through educational experiences, they also have underlying developmental components, of which educators must be aware if they are to address the perceived skill deficits of new graduates. Although writing is an important goal for senior capstones in its own right, this chapter argues that it can also be a powerful facilitator of personal and intellectual development in college seniors. To that end, some of the most common developmental challenges students face as they make the transition out of college are highlighted. In addition, the chapter examines the ways in which the kinds of writing assignments currently used in senior capstones may facilitate growth in these areas and suggests other writing experiences that might further support students' development.

### Critical Developmental Tasks in the Senior Year

The discussion of development draws on the work of a number of well-known theorists in the higher education literature, including William Perry, Arthur Chickering and Linda Reisser, Karen Kitchener and Patricia King, and Marcia Baxter Magolda. Several of these theories grew out of research on largely White, male undergraduates attending college in the 1960s. While subsequent research has refined these early theories and new models have emerged to describe the developmental experiences of women and underrepresented student populations, the most commonly referenced theories of student development may be limited in their ability to describe the experiences of many of today's college seniors. Therefore, this discussion is not meant to be predictive or prescriptive. Rather, descriptions of development are offered to provide instructors with some insight into how the challenges students may be navigating during the last quarter of their undergraduate education intersect with and impact important learning outcomes of senior capstone experiences.

Further, a full treatment of their theories is beyond the scope of this chapter. Rather, the chapter examines those developmental tasks that are both most salient for college seniors and most intertwined with the goals and purposes of capstone experiences. These tasks have been organized into three overarching areas of development—intrapersonal, interpersonal, and epistemological. Despite this organizing scheme, it is important to acknowledge the highly interconnected nature of development. For example, a person's epistemological development (i.e., how he or she makes meaning or justifies beliefs) has a very clear impact on self-definition (i.e., identity development). At the same time, interpersonal development—or the ability to acknowledge the perspectives of diverse others—is intertwined with epistemological development.

## Intrapersonal Development: Who Am I?

It is not surprising that students nearing the end of their college careers are concerned with answering the question, Who am I?[3] Whether they are traditional-aged students who will be entering the workforce for the first time or adult learners preparing for re-entry, students will grapple with issues related to personal identity and values and strategies for balancing these with evolving social norms. While faculty may protest that such concerns are outside the scope of the academic sphere, there is some indication that employers may be looking to colleges to offer more support and guidance to students in their intrapersonal development. Hart Research Associates (2010) reported that 70% of employers responding to a survey about college learning felt that institutions needed to place greater emphasis on the ability to innovate and be creative; 75% wanted to see more attention paid to the ability to connect choices and actions to ethical decisions. Helping students navigate several interrelated developmental tasks

---

[3]The framework for this discussion draws heavily on Marcia Baxter Magolda's (2001) holistic description of development in *Making Their Own Way: Narratives for Transforming Higher Education to Promote Self-Development.*

(e.g., establishing identity, developing purpose, gaining integrity, forming commitments) may increase their likelihood of achieving these important learning outcomes.

A number of factors—including vocation or career, social group membership (i.e., race or ethnicity, gender, sexual orientation), social roles (i.e., parent, spouse, or significant other)—intersect to form a core identity. According to Chickering and Reisser (1993), establishing identity involves managing a number of interconnected tasks, including developing comfort with one's body and appearance; comfort with one's gender and sexual orientation; a sense of self in social, historical, and cultural contexts; clarification of self-concept through roles and lifestyle; a sense of self in response to feedback from valued others; self-acceptance and self-esteem; and personal stability and integration. Jones and McEwen (2000) theorized that a person's various social identities formed a series of overlapping spheres around the core personal identity. At any given moment, individual social identities may have greater salience (i.e., move closer to the core) determined in part by the person's context (i.e., family background, sociocultural conditions, current experiences, career decisions, and life planning). To the extent that senior capstones sometimes play a socializing function for a discipline or profession, they may provide important sites for students to test the fit between their identities and the norms and values of that community.

Yet, an individual's cognitive complexity may influence his or her perceptions of fit within a particular disciplinary community. Abes, Jones, and McEwen (2007) suggested individuals who engage in what they call formulaic meaning making (akin to Perry's dualism or King and Kitchener's pre-reflective thinking) may assign greater salience to contextual influences than internal criteria when establishing identity. As individuals develop more sophisticated strategies for making sense of the world around them, they may become more adept at resisting externally imposed stereotypes. For example, a woman enrolled in an engineering seminar may struggle with feelings of fit (i.e., adopting engineer as part of her core identity) if she is locked into stereotypic views of appropriate careers for women. Collier's research (2000) proposed that capstone courses may help students navigate these problems of fit by providing them with examples of concrete behaviors associated with a desired role and structured learning experiences that allow them to practice such behaviors. Having the opportunity to perform like an engineer and learning that successful performance is grounded in behaviors and knowledge rather than personal characteristics, such as gender, challenge formulaic thinking and help students move toward greater cognitive complexity.

At the same time that increasing cognitive complexity may free some students from debilitating stereotypes, it may feel like a threat to identity for others. Perry (1968/1999) suggested the emergence of relativism may lead to a "loss of identity" (p. 149) at times. That is, if the senior capstone is successful in enhancing students' critical thinking, it may trigger a crisis for some students. For example, a young man planning to pursue a graduate degree in the sciences may find that deeply held religious beliefs are seemingly at odds with the values of the scientific community he hopes to enter. He may struggle with how to reconcile two highly valued aspects of his identity—person of faith and budding scientist. Faculty can be supportive of students by providing forums for them to examine these emerging intrapersonal conflicts within the senior capstone. Writing is one way to explore the boundaries of these conflicts—not necessarily to resolve them, but to grapple with the significance of embracing new perspectives.

Perry (1968/1999) suggested one way to ameliorate the threat to identity caused by emerging relativism is to make commitments or conscious choices about where to invest one's energy. The notion of evolving commitments is closely related to Chickering and Reisser's (1993) developing purpose and developing integrity. They defined developing purpose as "an increasing ability to be intentional, to assess interests and options, to clarify goals, to make plans, and to persist despite obstacles" (p. 50). Chickering and Reisser theorized that developing integrity proceeds through three sequential, but overlapping stages, with individuals moving "away from automatic application of uncompromising beliefs" (p. 51) toward greater respect for others' perspectives and conscious affirmation of core values. In the final stage, individuals develop congruence as they begin to match their "personal values with socially responsible behavior" (p. 51).

While developing purpose clearly has implications with respect to career decisions, issues related to purpose and integrity also shape an individual's career readiness (e.g., the ability to connect choices and actions to ethical decisions). Thus, the senior capstone must move beyond simply providing opportunities for students to test vocational fit or prepare career-related documents (e.g., cover letters, résumés) to engaging students in learning experiences that require them to be self-directed and respond to real-world problems where different value systems may be in conflict. For example, Peterson, Phillips, Bacon, and Machunda (2011) described a senior seminar for social work majors connected to a field internship. In the seminar, students identified and evaluated best practices in the human services literature. Working with the field supervisor, they came up with a plan for applying this literature in the internship setting. At the end of the seminar, they reflected on this application of the literature to practice in a formal presentation. Such an experience not only provides students with information about career fit but also gives them insight into how social workers use evidence to make decisions in practice settings.

### Interpersonal Development: What Is My Relationship to Others?

Interpersonal development involves discerning the answer to the question, How do I want to relate to other people? Two of Chickering and Reisser's (1993) vectors—moving through autonomy toward interdependence and developing mature interpersonal relationships—are useful to consider with respect to the senior capstone. Chickering and Reisser suggested the successful resolution of questions surrounding autonomy means "learning to function with relative self-sufficiency, to take responsibility for pursuing self-chosen goals, and to be less bound by others' opinions" (p. 47). Thus, achieving autonomy involves both emotional and instrumental independence. According to Chickering and Reisser, instrumental independence involves problem-solving skills or the ability to think critically and translate thought into action. Senior capstones that involve significant inquiry learning (i.e., student-conceived-and-designed research projects) may facilitate the development of instrumental independence, provided students feel adequate support from faculty, advisors, and peers throughout the experience. Conferences, written feedback on proposals and early drafts, and opportunities to exchange and comment on drafts with peers are other ways to help students navigate this developmental task within the senior capstone.

Closely connected to realizing autonomy (and theorized as building on it developmentally) is establishing mature interpersonal relationships, which Chickering and Reisser (1993) suggested encompasses both the capacity for intimacy and tolerance for and appreciation of differences, with the latter having greater relevance for the senior capstone. Research suggests men and women may differ in their ability to tolerate difference or engage a variety of perspectives. Foubert, Nixon, Sisson, and Barnes (2005) found "women not only were more tolerant than men throughout their college experience, but women also were more tolerant at the beginning of their college experience than men were after 4 years of development during college" (p. 469). Baxter Magolda's (1992, 1999) epistemological reflection model provides some insight into these differences with its inclusion of gender-related patterns of justifying knowledge assumptions.[4] For example, in transitional knowing (akin to Perry's multiplicity), men may be more likely to engage in debate to resolve uncertainty while women may be more apt to work toward building rapport to ensure their ideas are heard. Similarly, because the primary focus for male independent knowers (similar to Perry's relativism or King and Kitchener's quasi-reflective thinking) is on sharing their own ideas, they "sometimes struggled to listen carefully to other voices" (Baxter Magolda, 1999, p. 49). Women, on the other hand, tended to balance "thinking for themselves and engaging the views of others" (Baxter Magolda, 1999, p. 56).

Thus, gender-related patterns of knowledge justification may explain why men appear to be less tolerant of difference than their female peers throughout their college experience. Yet, 71% of employers wanted to see greater emphasis on teamwork skills and the ability to collaborate with others in diverse group settings (Hart Research Associates, 2010). To ensure that both men and women are developing an appropriate skill set in this area, faculty in senior capstones should design learning experiences that incorporate a variety of perspectives on issues within the discipline and/or real-world problems. Moreover, those experiences should be structured in such a way that they encourage consensus building and looking for common ground rather than debating and delineating differences. Collaborative writing assignments, especially when they ask students to research and evaluate possible solutions to a problem, may be one way to facilitate growth in this area.

### Epistemological Development: How Do I Know?

As should be clear by now, the questions—Who am I? and What is my relationship to others?—are inextricably linked to the question, How do I know? Yet, this area of development has perhaps the most immediate relevance for the senior capstone given the importance placed on analytical and critical-thinking skills within these courses. Two theories—Perry's (1968/1999) scheme of intellectual and ethical development and King and Kitchener's reflective judgment model (1994)—suggest the basic trajectory of epistemological development during the college years.

---

[4]While particular patterns were more commonly associated with one gender, they were not necessarily exclusive to that gender. Moreover, Baxter Magolda (1992) argued they should be seen as "different but equally valid approaches to knowing" (p. 37).

Most traditional-aged students enter college assuming there are answers (in most cases, one right answer) to all questions and that authorities (e.g., teachers, parents, religious leaders) know those answers. This epistemological stage has been variously referred to as dualism (Perry, 1968/1999), pre-reflective thinking (King & Kitchener, 1994), and absolute knowing (Baxter Magolda, 1992, 1999). Pre-reflective thinkers are unlikely to examine their beliefs and may justify them based on their alignment with an external authority figure (King & Kitchener, 1994). Yet, encounters with divergent views eventually lead students to conclude that some knowledge may be uncertain. Despite this evolution in thinking, late pre-reflective thinkers, or Perry's multiplists, believe authorities will eventually find the answer to questions that are currently unknown. Until such a time, students frequently rely on personal beliefs (still largely defined by external others) to make decisions (King & Kitchener, 1994). A certain cynicism may accompany this shift, as Perry suggested that students view the introduction of uncertainty as either a failure of authorities to play "their mediational role" (Perry, 1968/1999, p. 81) or as a mere instructional tool designed to help students learn to think for themselves. As such, diverse perspectives are "a mere procedural impediment intervening between taking up a problem and finding *the* answer" (Perry, 1968/1999, p. 87). Few college seniors will still be working within this set of assumptions, but those who are would probably struggle with assignments requiring them to define the parameters of a problem or their response to it. Further, these students are likely to express frustration with more open-ended assignments and may have difficulty getting started on the independent research projects that are a staple of many senior capstones.

Faced with increasingly divergent perspectives and vexing problems, individuals may begin to assume that knowledge is largely uncertain and evidence used to justify claims is primarily idiosyncratic—a stage of development labeled quasi-reflective thinking by King and Kitchener (1994; late multiplicity in Perry's scheme). In the vacuum created by a fallible authority, Perry (1968/1999) suggested the problem occupying students at this point in their epistemological development is how to judge the answers to questions when one answer appears as good as any other. For example, early quasi-reflective thinkers may not readily distinguish among an article appearing in a refereed journal, a blog post, or a popular magazine with respect to their potential contributions to a scholarly debate. Exercises that ask students to assess and respond to a variety of sources will equip them with a set of criteria necessary to begin weighing evidence and use it more effectively in support of their own beliefs.

As students wrestle with the uncertainty of knowledge, they may come to the realization that knowledge is contextual, which leads to using context-specific rules for inquiry and interpretation (i.e., late quasi-reflective thinking, King & Kitchener, 1994). Developing the capacity to bring evidence from different contexts to bear in considering ill-structured problems facilitates reflective thinking. Here, answers to vexing problems are constructed based on the best available evidence from a range of perspectives and contexts. Moreover, answers are open to re-evaluation as new evidence becomes available (King & Kitchener, 1994).

The challenge for students in thinking reflectively is two-fold: developing (a) a breadth of knowledge of the perspectives and evidence available across a range of contexts and (b) the skills necessary to evaluate that information critically. Collaborative projects may be particularly useful in meeting this challenge—especially if group members are assigned to research and represent different perspectives on an issue. The collective offers the breadth of knowledge that individual students may not be able to develop on their own while group members challenge each other to consider the information brought forward, particularly if it would demand a re-examination of an emerging consensus on the issue.

Research using the Reflective Judgment Interview (King & Kitchener, 2002, 2004) suggests that epistemological development in college plateaus about Stage 4, early quasi-reflective thinking. In fact, students appear to gain only about a half a stage in the move from pre-reflective to quasi-reflective thinking from the first year of college to the senior year. Thus, many students in the senior capstone may struggle when asked to engage in complex analysis or synthesis that requires drawing on a range of contexts to respond to ill-structured problems. Importantly, King and Kitchener (1994) suggested epistemological development proceeds in a wave-like rather than stair-step fashion, with students exhibiting characteristics of several stages at any one time. Optimal performance, or the leading edge of the wave, is the "upper limit of the person's general information-processing capacity" (Kitchener & Fischer, quoted in King & Kitchener, 1994, p. 29). According to King and Kitchener (1994), an individual's capacity to perform at optimal levels depends on a number of factors, including the difficulty of the task, the amount of practice offered, and the clarity of feedback provided. Thus, while students in the senior capstone may struggle with tasks that require reflective thinking, they are very likely capable of engaging in reflective thinking with the appropriate scaffolding and support.

For example, students likely will struggle when asked to defend their argument as being better (i.e., more reflective of current understandings, based on a more sound research methodology) than those of others—especially if the others are published researchers. King and Kitchener (1994) suggested instructors can help students succeed in this task by modeling strategies for defending points of view without dismissing or appearing intolerant of other positions on an issue. Using cases studies in the discipline to demonstrate how points of views have evolved over time as more evidence became available or how advances in technology allowed for different kinds of questions to be answered can help students learn to position their own arguments successfully. McElroy (1997) advocated for student-instructor conferences during which the two collaborate on the interpretation of student-collected data. He noted that conferences offer students "opportunities for discovering new explanations, for critiquing and modifying the methodology, and even for reformulating the hypothesis and testing procedures" (p. 34).

## Writing as a Facilitator of Student Development

As suggested above, faculty have a number of strategies available to help students navigate critical developmental tasks in the senior year. This section presents some of the more common writing activities and assignments incorporated into the senior capstone and suggests where such assignments might work to facilitate the personal and intellectual development of college students. In addition, recommendations are offered for some types of writing not currently common in capstone experiences that might be incorporated to support both developmental and learning outcomes associated with the course. Many of these assignments and strategies are addressed in greater detail later in the book.

### Integrative and Inquiry-Based Writing

As noted in chapter 1, the most frequently described writing assignments within the senior capstone were reports of original research and traditional academic research papers designed for synthesis and integration. In addition to these library-based research papers, other integrative writing assignments are used in the seminar. Drawing on readings, class discussions, dialogic log responses, and ideas generated in the course, students in a senior seminar for English majors at Radford University produced a 15-20-page essay in response to the question, What is English? (Baker, 1997). Similarly, a senior seminar for psychology majors at Loyola University of Chicago asked students to write a 5-10-page paper synthesizing and integrating their reading, discussions, and learning experiences within the course (Zechmeister & Reich, 1994).

At a minimum, such assignments should promote quasi-reflective thinking in students, for in order to develop successful synthesis and integration essays, they must be able to see the larger contexts within which different perspectives in the discipline exist. When well designed, such tasks might promote reflective thinking. To help students review and reflect on their disciplinary learning while in college, King and Kitchener (1994) suggested the following assignment: "Provide your own organization of a given field of study (for example, concept mapping of a course or a discipline), with explicit reference to the interrelationships between elements" (p. 254).

Inquiry-based writing assignments (i.e., the senior research paper or project, cases, or problem-based learning) are by their very nature ill-structured problems in that students must not only define the parameters of the question they want to explore but also the strategies for examining the question and the likely forms their answer might take. As such, these projects are highly likely to give students practice in reflective thinking. At Cornell College, students in a sociology senior seminar drew on library research, interviews with policy makers, document analysis, and observations from internship settings to write a 30-page research paper analyzing a social problem and the policy existing to address it (Carlson & Peterson, 1993). Similarly, Chew, McInnis-Bowers, Cleveland, and Drewer (1996) described a case approach in a business administration capstone at Birmingham-Southern College: "These students interactively combine their competencies from their individual specialties [e.g., management, marketing, finance] to assess, define, and solve the multidimensional, complex, ill-defined problems presented in the case studies" (Collaborative Learning section, para. 1). The case approach has the added benefit of supporting students' interpersonal development, as they must learn to appreciate the diverse expertise and viewpoints of their classmates to formulate an effective resolution.

### *Exploratory Writing*

Much of the writing in the senior capstone involves long, formal academic pieces. While these writing assignments can facilitate epistemological development, students may struggle to produce high-quality responses to such assignments without adequate support. In some cases, students who do not routinely function as reflective thinkers may not produce the thoughtful, well-developed arguments demanded by integrative and inquiry-based writing assignments. At other times, the move to more complex ways of thinking about issues and articulating solutions may lead to disorganization, an absence of appropriate support, and unclear phrasing. For example, a study of high school and college writers (Hays, Brandt, & Chantry, 1988) revealed that students who rated higher on the Perry scale produced papers that were not so clearly focused and more likely to be "filled with tangled syntax" (p. 413) than those of their peers who scored slightly lower on the scale. Informal or exploratory writing assignments are useful in responding to both issues—that is, they can be used to offer students practice in thinking more complexly and to provide a space for working out ideas that can be later transformed into more polished prose.

Exploratory writing can take a variety of forms, including brief reading responses, journals, blogs, or short memos, which allows students to reflect and focus their attention on specific elements that are confusing, such as a controversial line of research in the discipline. Hays (1995) suggested that opportunities for exploratory writing, specifically a journal, help students see themselves as knowers, and validating students' capacity to know is a key principle in supporting their ongoing epistemological development (Baxter Magolda, 2001). Short, in-class exploratory writing assignments (i.e., quick-writes) can become the foundation for purposeful small-group discussions leading to student-generated interpretations and solutions to student-identified problems. Such conversations promote both interpersonal and epistemological development by exposing students to diverse perspectives and by embedding them in an environment in which authority and expertise are shared in the mutual construction of knowledge among peers (Baxter Magolda, 2001, pp. xx-xxi). A second quick-write following the group discussion allows students to explore new insights and to reach greater clarity in their thinking and writing. In describing his action research study on a college literature course, Kroll (1992) found that reflective journal writing, to which the instructor responded, and peer group discussions were two of the most effective strategies in fostering reflective thinking.

Exploratory writing assignments also can help bridge the gap between epistemological and intrapersonal development. Given the complex and interrelated nature of development, such assignments can be especially helpful for students who are planning to make the transition out of college. In identifying appropriate writing assignments in a senior capstone in sociology, Wagenaar (1993) noted that a student might use a journal to examine his or her intellectual and sociological development, including "reflections on the discipline, questions that emerge, analyses of everyday experiences, and letters to the instructor" (p. 213). Wei et al. (2007) described a capstone course for information systems and technology management majors at Syracuse University that incorporated weekly journal assignments in which students recorded "their personal reflections, contributions, and learning experiences undertaken in the previous week(s)" (p. 129). Journal writing also might be an important counterpoint to more formal academic writing. Commenting on Kroll's (1992) efforts to increase reflective thinking in a course on the literature of the Vietnam War, King and Kitchener (1994) stated,

> Having students wrestle with such issues through reflective journals prior to submitting formal papers yielded a wealth of information not only about what students were drawing upon as the basis for their beliefs but what questions, personal issues, or emotional responses were keeping them from making a fully reasoned judgment. (p. 241)

Thus, exploratory writing can be an important metacognitive tool for students to examine how questions of identity, values, and belief shape their approaches to knowledge construction.

Several senior seminars included intellectual autobiography assignments (e.g., Smith, 1993; Troyer, 1993). Such an assignment might ask students to trace their intellectual development in the major and throughout college or to explore emerging tensions between deeply held personal beliefs and the epistemological stance(s) of the disciplinary or professional community. Finally, the intellectual autobiography also could be a forum for exploring the student's readiness for graduate school or a career. In this case, students might respond to questions such as, How have my college experiences prepared me for work or graduate school? In what areas do I feel unprepared? and How should I address those gaps through my current research projects, internships, or other academic experiences?

### Career-Related Writing

While writing assignments in the senior capstone are overwhelmingly academic, career-related writing assignments also can be important vehicles for supporting student learning and development. Career-related assignments might be thought of in two ways: as (a) documents supporting a job search or graduate school application and (b) artifacts of workplace writing. While cover letters and résumés seem like highly utilitarian texts on the surface, the process of creating them can help students identify and articulate important vocational values. When developing these documents, students may be prompted to examine more closely the fit between their values and those of the career or disciplinary field they hope to enter. As such, résumés, cover letters, statements of intent, and similar documents can facilitate the development of purpose and identity for students preparing to leave college.

Assignments that ask students to produce samples of workplace writing (e.g., memoranda, technical manuals, policy briefs, project proposals) help them develop valuable skills and acclimate them to disciplinary and professional conventions. However, such assignments are also valuable tools for facilitating epistemological development, especially when they ask students to respond to open-ended or ill-structured problems.

## Conclusion

This volume is designed to facilitate the incorporation of writing in the senior capstone to achieve a variety of important learning and developmental outcomes. The next chapter offers general guidance on the how, what, and why of writing instruction in the senior seminar. Chapters 4 through 8 describe specific strategies and assignments. We close this chapter with some recommendations for using writing to support intrapersonal, interpersonal, and epistemological development in the senior capstone.

- Students typically operate within a developmental range, especially with respect to critical thinking. To help students achieve their optimal performance, faculty can provide guidelines, low-stakes opportunities for practice, and specific feedback. Modeling also may help students achieve optimal performance. Instructors can show how they use evidence to make judgments. They also can demonstrate their discipline's critical-reading process, emphasizing connections among reading, thinking, and writing. McElroy (1997) described a capstone course in economics in which the instructor wrote alongside students, "creating his or her own research paper and presenting mini-drafts of each component about one week before similar student assignments are due" (p. 33).

- Faculty also can capitalize on students' developmental range by building on familiar critical-thinking skills, such as summary, to develop more complex skills, such as synthesis. To do this effectively, faculty can begin by identifying the particular cognitive skills needed to complete a task and then assigning reading, thinking, and writing tasks in a rough developmental sequence. A geochemistry instructor at Rice University used sequenced reading and writing tasks to teach students to read critically and evaluate published scientific literature simultaneously and found the process helped them develop those skills as well as reach their own conclusions in a critical analysis of the research (C. Masiello, personal communication, May 24, 2012).

- To facilitate development, assignments have to be challenging enough to move students past their typical level of functioning. With respect to developing reflective thinking, faculty must design assignments that encourage students to consider and evaluate multiple perspectives on their topics. Further, writing assignments should incorporate ill-structured problems so that students can practice bringing evidence from multiple contexts to bear in developing and defending potential solutions.

- Perry (1968/1999) noted that transition from one frame of reference to the other (e.g., from dualism to multiplicity, from multiplicity to relativism) can be emotionally challenging for students. To help them persist and continue to take intellectual risks, faculty members can demonstrate respect for students' current perspectives and beliefs. Opportunities for personal reflection through journals may help some students deal with the emotional fallout of increasing cognitive complexity.

- Learning to work as part of a team made up of diverse individuals is an important workplace skill, but it also has implications for epistemological development. Opportunities for collaborative writing projects and peer review of drafts help students learn to value their classmates' perspectives and expertise in relation to their own interests and needs.

# Chapter 3

## Guidelines for Writing Instruction in the Senior Capstone

As seen in chapter 1, the senior capstone places a strong emphasis on writing, with many of these courses designed to help students produce a major senior project typically presented both orally and in writing. Thus, much of the writing in senior capstones may be conceived as a single type of writing—that is, academic research—and may not accurately reflect the reality of writing in professions outside academe. Further, such a narrow conceptualization of writing and writing assignments does not capitalize on the full potential of writing to support the learning and development of students at the end of the undergraduate experience. This chapter draws on the *NCTE Beliefs About the Teaching of Writing* (2004), a document that distills the basic philosophy teachers of English have about writing to the following 11 principles:

1. Everyone has the capacity to write; writing can be taught; and teachers can help students become better writers.

2. People learn to write by writing.

3. Writing is a process.

4. Writing is a tool for thinking.

5. Writing grows out of many purposes.

6. Conventions of finished and edited texts are important to readers and, therefore, to writers.

7. Writing and reading are related.

8. Writing has a complex relationship to talk.

9. Literate practices are embedded in complicated social relationships.

10. Composing occurs in different modalities and technologies.

11. Assessment of writing involves complex, informed, human judgment (NCTE, 2004).

While the NCTE statement is broadly focused to encompass writing instruction at the primary, secondary, and postsecondary level, here we recast a number of these general principles to help instructors think more expansively about the uses of writing in a capstone course. This chapter is designed to offer general guidance on how to incorporate and support the development of writing in a senior capstone. The remainder of the book provides more focused suggestions for incorporating specific kinds of writing assignments and activities into capstone courses.

## Everyone Has the Capacity to Write

The central premise of the NCTE statement is the idea that everyone can learn to write. While writing is frequently cast as a creative endeavor, it is also a skill. Like most skills, proficiency requires opportunities for practice and feedback. Instructors in the senior capstone may feel ill-equipped to provide the support and feedback needed for the development of basic writing skills, yet as faculty, they are likely fairly accomplished writers and well versed in the expectations of writing within a particular discipline. They also may have insights into the preferred standards of written communication in government, business, medicine, and other fields outside academe. To that end, they have a useful set of skills and experiences to share with their students. Faculty can model their own approaches to research and writing for their students and, where possible, write with their students. As described in chapter 2, McElroy (1997) offered a useful strategy for mentoring student writers this way.

## People Learn to Write by Writing

The development of writing skills requires practice. For students to gain maximum fluency, they should have the opportunity to write both in and out of class and for a variety of audiences and purposes. Yet, much of the writing students do in college is limited to the standard genres of essay exam, research paper, and canned lab report. Moving beyond these traditional assignments to include those that expose students "to the worlds of writing through which people work and live" (Russell, 2001, p. 287) is a way to introduce both practice and varied intents.

For example, students might be challenged to move from academic to action genres (e.g., letters to newspapers, guest editorials, opinion pieces to government officials or administrators). Students who write as part of a service-learning program in their senior capstones can create documents for organizations that people actually use, such as guides, technical manuals, or newsletters. Jolliffe (2001) reported that students in his service-based writing course produced a manual for developing a summer reading program, a teacher's guide for working with students with hearing impairments, and a web page for parents whose children have eating disorders. While the ultimate goal of the senior capstone might be the completion of an independent research project or paper, instructors could also investigate the ways in which the kinds of writing students do for themselves (e.g., e-mails, journals, blogs, Tweets, text messages) can be appropriated for academic purposes.

In addition, instructors should consider how students could explore the concepts, questions, and theories of a discipline in genres more representative of the workplace (e.g., memoranda, proposals, reports, internal and external communications). Practicing reading and writing in genres specific to a chosen field can help develop a sense of membership to a professional community (Miller, 1994). The reproducible patterns within a discipline-specific genre manage, shape, and structure communication, while recognition of the genre's conventions signals community participation and membership (Miller, 1994). Jolliffe (2001) also noted there is a relationship between learning to write in a particular discipline-based genre and forming an identity as a knower or professional in that field.

Having an awareness of genre possibilities allows students to evaluate the interactions among language use, culture, and power as well as consider how language creates action in society. Further, writing in a specific genre can provide a structure or tools to solve problems that new information or understanding may create. Similarly, students may find their thinking reshaped as the conventions of the genre narrow rhetorical decisions to be made (Jolliffe, 2001). Always evolving, genres develop through regular use for similar purposes in fluid social contexts (Devitt, 2000). The ways in which genres change through the interactions among writers, readers, and contexts make them richly loaded with cultural, historical, and social values (Devitt, 2000). Practice with multiple genres not only broadens students' writing abilities but also can support cognitive development by providing opportunities to reframe, restructure, and rethink knowledge (Bazerman, 2009).

## Writing Is a Process

The writing process is not linear; rather, it is a complex movement toward a final product, including a "repertory of routines, skills, strategies, and practices, for generating, revising, and editing different kinds of texts" (NCTE, 2004, Writing Is a Process section, para. 1). The greater exposure students have to writing, the more opportunity they have to develop this repertory. Despite the emphasis on process in writing instruction, many students may still view writing as the act of transcribing fully formed ideas onto the page. When they experience difficulty developing those ideas, writing stalls or fails to launch altogether. Instructors of senior capstones can emphasize the writing process as a series of problems to be solved, using rhetorical strategies to analyze, develop, and organize the context, purpose, and audience of documents. Emphasizing problem solving in the writing process helps students develop independence, self-confidence, and creativity by pushing them to answer their own questions about planning, designing, and composing their documents, rather than depending on templates, models, or a set of explicit instructions. For example, when students ask, "How long does it have to be?" instructors should respond, "How long do you think it needs to be?"

It is also important for students to understand that writing involves drafting, rethinking, revising, and drafting again. Though students may view requirements to create multiple drafts as busy work (and faculty may see it an unnecessary addition to their workload), there is great value in helping students understand the fluidity of texts.

### Invention: Ways to Begin Thinking, Writing, and Reflecting

Invention consists of the ways in which ideas are discovered through writing. While typically conceived as a first step in the writing process, in reality writers engage in invention at all points along the way, particularly when they sense a need for greater development of an idea or concept. A wide range of in- and out-of-class activities can help students identify and narrow topics for writing or more fully develop writing projects already in process. Activities might include

- small-group discussions or brainstorming sessions;
- concept maps or cluster diagrams;

- cubing, or writing on a single topic or issue from a variety of perspectives;
- listing;
- outlining; and
- freewriting, or writing for a set period of time without worrying about correctness, completeness, or organization.

The exploratory writing assignments previously mentioned and described in greater depth in chapter 4 (i.e., brief reading responses, journals, blogs, memos, and personal reflections on the course) may also serve as an incubator for longer, more fully developed texts.

Ideally, the early stages of a writing project will incorporate a range of invention activities and not just a single 20-minute freewrite completed in class sometime before the first draft is due. Successive invention activities build on and refine the ideas developed earlier. Alternately, separate invention strategies can be used to develop specific sections of a larger writing project. For example, if students are completing an independent research project for a senior capstone, they could construct a concept map based on their reading of related research and theoretical pieces as a precursor to drafting a literature review. Similarly, once data analysis has been completed, students might draft a memo or a journal entry describing the findings (e.g., were they as expected, why or why not?). Students' work here will lay the groundwork for their discussion section.

Instructors can choose not to grade or offer feedback on invention activities, responding to them only as complete or incomplete, as part of the work that builds the larger product. Or, they might assess them broadly as exemplary, satisfactory, or incomplete, noting students' effort and commitment to the early stages of the writing process. In fact, offering feedback at this point may be counterproductive, as the image of the faculty member as audience may deter students from taking risks in their exploration of ideas and, thus, limit or foreclose possibilities for the future (Elbow, 1987).

### *Drafting*

After students generate ideas, they are ready to review their freewriting, notes, and journal responses, and integrate material into their drafts, rephrasing as needed. The goal of writing at this point is developing a full text geared to a specific purpose and targeting a particular audience. If students are expected to write in a certain genre (e.g., social science research article, business prospectus, technical manual), instructors can provide structure to the drafting process by identifying the order, purpose, and typical content of the major sections of the text. Students may find it helpful to insert these section headings into their documents to focus early efforts. Writing in response to such headings frees students to develop the sections of the text with which they feel most confident first and come back to other sections once their ideas have ripened.

Unlike writing produced during invention, student drafts are ready for feedback. Instructors may choose to read them and offer formative responses. They might assign grades appropriate for that stage of the writing process or simply note whether they represent satisfactory or unsatisfactory progress. However, faculty do not have to be the only readers of student work. Peer review of drafts can be beneficial for all students. The writer has an opportunity to see how a real reader responds to his or her work and receives valuable feedback to help reshape that work to reach the reader more effectively. On the other hand, the reader (who is also a writer) sees how his or her peers are managing similar rhetorical challenges and may gain new insights for structuring his or her own text.

Students, and sometimes faculty, may be reluctant to invest time in peer review because they wonder whether novices in the discipline and inexperienced writers can be effective reviewers for classmates' work. In examining peer review among high school seniors, Simmons (2003) concluded that students could indeed offer useful feedback on their peers' writing, provided they had explicit instruction. For example, instructors can increase the likelihood that students will offer effective feedback by modeling strategies for offering specific praise, demonstrating understanding, asking questions, and making suggestions (Simmons, 2003). Because many faculty are engaged in academic publishing in their disciplines, they might choose to model these strategies for students by walking through their review of a manuscript or by sharing with students a useful review they received on their own work. Students can gain practice with these strategies by using them to respond to course readings before reviewing peer drafts.

In addition to modeling and practice, careful sequencing of peer review tasks may increase their effectiveness. At the beginning of a course when students are working with new material and ideas, peer review might focus on simpler tasks (e.g., summary) before moving on to analysis and assessment. As a course proceeds, instructors can increase the critical thinking required during peer review by asking students to respond to higher level rhetorical choices, such as how writers organize and interweave different kinds of supporting information and arguments. Alternately, peer review responses can be tailored to specific stages of the writing process. When working with middle drafts, students could help each other expand ideas, flesh out explanations, and incorporate examples to support the paper's primary argument. If students are working with advanced drafts, they might evaluate the use of research to support assertions or claims or check adherence to disciplinary citation and formatting styles.

### Revising and Editing

While in reality revising and editing happen throughout the writing process, it is sometimes useful to make the strategies that accompany these activities more explicit for students and to suggest a logical timeline for focusing their attentions on these activities during the writing process. For example, many students may understand revising and editing to mean essentially the same thing, yet revising is focused problem solving (Walvoord & McCarthy, 1990) during which writers consider whether the draft has satisfied rhetorical goals regarding purpose, audience, scope, content, and organization. Editing, on the other hand, involves word and sentence-level changes that impact style, clarity, and tone. Thus, it makes little sense for a student to invest energy in closely editing a paragraph that ultimately may be cut from the paper. Sequencing the final steps in manuscript development (i.e., revising, editing, and proofreading) and defining the primary objective of each step clarify the process for students.

The revising process demands a complex set of higher level reading and thinking skills, which students have to develop and apply effectively. They must read to identify specific rhetorical elements in their writing, review and assess these elements, analyze problems in their writing, and design a revision plan. Writing handbooks abound with helpful heuristics students can use to identify revision goals. For example, Ruszkiewicz, Friend, and Hairston (2008) identified six areas for revision (i.e., focus, purpose, proportion, audience, organization, and content) with questions to help guide students as they evaluate their writing. In addition to these more generic questions, faculty might use queries reflecting the standards for a specific genre within the discipline. Because many senior capstone courses ask students to develop pieces that can be submitted for publication, instructors may introduce the manuscript evaluation guidelines used by reviewers for select journals in the discipline to help students develop a revision plan. As noted above, responding to their peers' drafts will make students more adept at identifying these issues within their own drafts.

To be successful editors of their work, students must use specific strategies to locate, analyze, and correct errors; clarify phrasing; tighten expression; and adjust tone. Instructors in the senior capstone may feel that explicit instruction in correct usage is beyond the scope of the course, assuming that students should already have learned these skills. Yet, employers say that accuracy, clarity, and correctness do matter (Addison & McGee, 2010). As such, discussions about correcting errors can be connected to embracing a professional identity and developing skills that students will need to be successful in the workplace. Instructors can remind their students that proofreading thoroughly will help them give their writing a professional polish that reflects their authority and expertise—important elements of effective communication. Revising and editing to remove errors also demonstrates a concern with meeting the reader's needs. When writers are genuinely committed to the reader's experience, they will choose to meet the reader's needs through careful stylistic revisions, creating clear, correct, precise, and interesting prose. Moreover, writers who provide a straightforward reading experience are more likely to convince their readers that their arguments are reasonable.

Instructors of senior capstones also can view proofreading and editing as part of a critical assessment of language choices, rhetorical analysis, and decision making. For example, most style manuals strongly recommend active voice over passive voice, yet passive voice may be appropriate if the writer wants to emphasize the object acted upon rather that the actor (e.g., in writing the method section of a research study). Similarly, punctuation errors, such as the comma splice, are often the result of rhetorical decisions writers need to explore more fully. Fixing a comma splice requires more than just placing a dot over the comma to turn it into a semicolon. The writer must review the essential ideas in the two sentences joined by the comma and decide how to express a synthesis of those ideas more clearly or to better rhetorical effect. Should two shorter, punchier statements be created to emphasize one idea over another, or should a longer, more syntactically complex sentence be developed in which causal relationships are embedded through the use of subordinating conjunctions? Often, when writers make decisions about correcting punctuation or other surface errors, they are thinking about how they want the reader to react to the piece's voice and ideas. Rather than focusing on the correction of errors in student drafts either through peer review or instructor feedback, faculty can ask students to analyze the choices writers have made in assigned course readings and the effect of those choices on the reader.

## Writing Is a Tool for Thinking

Writing in undergraduate education, in general, and in the senior capstone, in particular, tends to focus on the production of an academic product. As such, there may be a limited view of the potential uses of writing (i.e., as a tool for assessing student learning), but as previously suggested, writing also can be an important source for learning and thinking. The process of writing helps students discover ideas that they may not have had when they began writing. Thus, writing can help students "to solve problems, to identify issues, to construct questions, to reconsider something one had already figured out, to try out a half-baked idea" (NCTE, 2004, Writing Is a Tool for Thinking section, para. 1). Yet, for writing to function this way, some of the writing assigned in the course has to be primarily for students (i.e., journals, reflections, observations). To the extent that informal, low-stakes writing assignments encourage exploration rather than movement toward a predetermined answer, these genres (e.g., blogs, posts to listservs or online discussion groups, reaction papers) can also help students synthesize important disciplinary concepts and develop critical-thinking skills.

## Writing Grows Out of Many Purposes, Using a Range of Genres

In *Beliefs About the Teaching of Writing*, NCTE (2004) identified a number of functions for writing that are congruent with the goals of the senior capstone, such as using writing to develop interpersonal relationships, engage in civic discourse, grow personally or spiritually, reflect on experiences, and communicate professionally. NCTE recommended students learn to use a variety of genres and modalities to convey these purposes. As Gere et al. (2008) noted, today's educators must prepare students for complex, digitized workplace writing that includes a broad range of genres (e.g., reports, memos, e-mails, presentations, notes) and help them become comfortable moving among these forms. Instructors of the senior capstone can include these various genres in both formal and informal writing activities following a developmental progression. For example, students can summarize notes from small-group discussions in electronic memos or e-mails, a process that requires them to listen actively during class discussions, generalize key points, and then synthesize ideas. In his study of co-op students, Brent (2012) found that such critical-thinking activities were valued in the workplace and that students were called on to multitask (i.e., write in different genres simultaneously).

Given the evolving nature of texts and business communications, students especially need experience in multimodal composition—that is, practice in embedding images, video, sound, and animation in documents that will be produced and distributed through digital media. Such assignments still require students to evaluate the rhetorical value of nonprint elements, strategies for embedding them effectively, and the result of those choices on the audience's experience of the text. For example, instructors might have students create digital portfolios, résumés, or electronic posters to accompany oral presentations using Prezi (www.prezi.com) or online blogging tools, such as WordPress (www.wordpress.com).

## Literate Practices Are Social in Nature

Inherent in every writing situation is a network of complex social relationships. As the 2004 NCTE report made clear, these relationships—especially in academic and work settings—are defined by power differentials:

> In every writing situation, the writer, the reader, and all relevant others live in a structured social order, where some people's words count more than others, where being heard is more difficult for some people than others, where some people's words come true and others' do not. (Literate Practices section, para. 1).

While it is impossible to erase the power differential between student and instructor, instructors can minimize it by entering into learning partnerships (Baxter Magolda & King, 2004). Sommers (2006) suggested instructors engage in a "partnership through feedback" (p. 250) when they offer genuine and specific comments that help students move forward with their writing.

Writing conferences have even greater potential for learning partnerships because students can dialogue with their instructor about ideas and revision plans. Faculty members facilitate such partnerships by treating their students as junior colleagues or developing experts. Bean (2011) suggested allowing students to set the agenda for conferences by asking questions, such as What do you think we should focus on today? What questions do you have about your draft? and What revision plans are you considering? Then, instructors should listen while students do 90% of the talking. Ideas can be mirrored back to students, followed by comments and questions, to help them develop explanatory depth in thought and writing. Reflecting ideas back to students gives them confidence that the faculty member has read their work, understood it, noticed the best ideas, and was enthusiastic about the topic. When instructors acknowledge students as developing experts, they can have much richer conversations about their topics as they share knowledge and opinions as collaborators, working with them to make new meaning out of their concerns (Thaiss & Zawacki, 2006). Beyond helping students grow as writers and thinkers, these partnerships or collaborations also support the development of self-authorship, or mature decision making, an important outcome for undergraduate education (Baxter Magolda & King, 2004).

## Assessing Writing Is a Complex Process

A position statement prepared by the Conference on College Composition and Communication (CCCC Committee on Assessment, 2006) emphasized the importance of authentic assessments that (a) are grounded in the local context in which the writing is created, (b) include reflections by the writer, (c) respect diversity and language variation, (d) provide multiple opportunities to demonstrate outcomes, and (e) value multiple genres and audiences. Above all, writing assessment must promote learning and be dedicated to illuminating what students do well (CCCC Committee on Assessment, 2006). Practices must be developed locally so that they integrate faculty values and beliefs about writing and provide opportunities for faculty development that emerge from assessment (CCCC Committee on Assessment, 2006). By bringing the voices of students, faculty, and administrators into the assessment program, these principles will help create practices that support the improvement of teaching and learning by revealing the full context of writing within an institution.

For senior capstones, instructors should base assessment strategies for each writing activity on factors related to general course goals, such as how the writing project promotes specific intellectual, academic, professional, and personal development, as well as on the typical features of good writing (e.g., voice, focus, organization, development, clarity). One of the major concerns faculty have about assessing writing is the amount of time it takes. Choosing to evaluate selected elements in each project, rather than trying to assess all aspects every time, will create a manageable workload and make assessment more valuable to students. By focusing their response in this way, instructors can guide students toward rereading for one or two major rhetorical elements (Sommers, 2006) and gradually introduce additional elements throughout the drafting process. The faculty member's reading then becomes more purposeful in general, and students discover for themselves other elements to revise. Thus, limiting responses encourages students to make their own choices in their writing.

Because there can be so many features to evaluate in any writing project, it is critical to have strategies to limit the evaluation process. The key to streamlining this process is for instructors to make choices about what, how, and when they assess student work. Developing and using rubrics to respond to student writing is one way to streamline this process. Condon (2011) criticized rubrics as having the potential to be reductive because they cannot capture the whole writing context, but he also noted rubrics can help communicate expectations, demystify the writing process, and reinforce a common language for talking about writing.

The Written Communication VALUE Rubric from AAC&U (Rhodes, 2010) offers the following benchmarks for assessing students' writing ability throughout college. Language in the rubric for the capstone benchmark might be particularly appropriate as a starting point for assessing student writing in the senior seminar, reflecting expectations for what students should be able to do as they leave college. The benchmarks are

- *context of and purpose for writing*—demonstrates a thorough understanding of context, audience, and purpose that is responsive to the assigned task(s) and focuses all elements of the work;

- *content development*—uses appropriate, relevant, and compelling content to illustrate mastery of the subject, conveying the writer's understanding and shaping the whole work;

- *genre and disciplinary conventions*—demonstrates detailed attention to and successful execution of a wide range of conventions particular to a specific discipline and/or writing task(s), including organization, content, presentation, formatting, and stylistic choices;

- *sources and evidence*—demonstrates skillful use of high-quality, credible, relevant sources to develop ideas that are appropriate for the discipline and genre of the writing; and

- *control of syntax and mechanics*—uses graceful language that skillfully communicates meaning to readers with clarity and fluency and is virtually error-free.

Rubrics can be analytic, holistic, generic, or task-specific, or some combination of these characteristics, depending upon the purpose of the response (Bean, 2011). Instructors will have to determine what they are responding to and why to develop the best rubric for any given writing project. However, if the assessment is to be instructive and ensure that all responses drive students toward improvement in their thinking and writing, then rubrics should always point toward revision suggestions. For this reason, rubrics are likely to be most useful in facilitating revision if they help describe what readers notice and experience, identify specific elements that are or are not working well, and point toward general strengths and areas to develop. For example, when students recognize that the lack of topic sentences throughout their essays creates confusion for the reader, they can choose to improve organization to make their argument more convincing.

In addition to using rubrics geared to the goals of the course and specific assignments, instructors may consider other options for managing the writing assessment load, such as

- choosing to grade only formal, revised prose;

- giving formative assessment orally, during conferences or small-group workshops;

- encouraging students to visit the campus writing center to receive formative feedback on early drafts; and

- using a portfolio review at the end of the course, assessing the selections the students choose for grading purposes.

### Involve Students in Assessment

Assessment is another area where instructors can enter into meaningful partnerships with students and help them feel more engaged with their writing projects. Involving students in the design of rubrics early in the semester will assist them in recognizing analytical connections among rhetorical elements. The rubric can be a checklist or composing guide for students while they are developing their documents and, when used to offer feedback, should lead to more effective revision. Questions that might guide small-group and whole-class discussion of rubric development include

- What main purpose does the writing project serve in this course?

- What are the most important critical-thinking skills (e.g., analysis, synthesis) that should be evident in this writing project?

- What writing elements (e.g., a clear thesis, explanation of the synthesis of ideas, direct topic sentences in each paragraph, analysis of the thesis's specific key points) are most important in helping to demonstrate these critical-thinking skills?

- What writing elements are most important to present a professional-looking document?

- What organizational features are most important to demonstrate awareness of disciplinary writing conventions?

- What elements in word choice are most important in creating a professional style?

- How should specific writing elements be weighted?

- How should critical thinking be judged and weighted?

- How should ideas be judged and weighted? and

- What role should the use of research play in the evaluation?

In some cases, students may be better prepared to respond to these questions with respect to the writing they will produce for the course if they have first applied them to published documents in the discipline.

### *Focus on Formative Assessment*

NCTE (2004) defines formative assessment as "provisional, ongoing, in-process judgments about what students know and what to teach next" ("Assessment of Writing Involves Complex, Informed Human Judgment," para. 3). Instructors can give formative feedback during conferences or conversations in class, or they can write comments on a rubric geared to a particular writing assignment or reflective of specific course learning outcomes. Formative responses help students know what they are doing well and what they can focus on during their next draft.

Huot (2002) refers to focusing on the next draft as instructive assessment, with instructors always pointing toward the upcoming writing activity and identifying strengths and weaknesses for students so they can continue building their skills by knowing what they are doing well and how they can change. The goal of responding instructively should be to deepen and expand ideas and explanations, always focusing first on ideas (Hodges, 1997). Even a final-draft assessment should help build a bridge toward the next writing context, whether that occurs within another course, at work, at home, or in graduate school.

As noted above, the instructor's voice does not have to be the only one in the review process; formative evaluation also can include self-review components. Such reflection helps students internalize their best writing practices and develop meaningful strategies for success (CCCC Committee on Assessment, 2006). Informal writing about peer-group responses; reflective letters about final drafts or portfolios; and e-mail messages to themselves, peer readers, or the instructor will help students gain insights useful in their future writing projects. For example, students might attach a self-assessment to a draft when turning it in. This assessment could be a rubric (Figure 3.1) or a more informal letter to the instructor describing what the student perceives as strengths or weaknesses and ongoing challenges at that point in the writing process. The instructor may use the self-assessment as a guide to issues to note when reviewing the draft, offering the student feedback specifically on areas he or she has identified as important.

1. Identify the strongest feature of this draft so far:

2. Describe the elements of this draft that you feel are most incomplete:

3. Identify any questions you have about this draft:

4. Required components are all present:      Yes      No
   a) Introduction: gives a brief overview of your study.
      Strong          Acceptable          Weak or Missing
   b) Explanation of your investigation: explains why you are studying this topic.
      Strong          Acceptable          Weak or Missing
   c) Methodology: explains how you studied this topic.
      Strong          Acceptable          Weak or Missing
   d) Data or other informational section: describes your findings.
      Strong          Acceptable          Weak or Missing
   e) Discussion: explains your ideas about your findings.
      Strong          Acceptable          Weak or Missing
   f) Conclusion and recommendations: identifies your overall ideas about your study, recommends future studies or actions on this topic.
      Strong          Acceptable          Weak or Missing

5. Describe your revision plans:

6. Instructor Response:
   a) You're doing your best work in this area:
   b) Concentrate your next effort strengthening this area:

*Figure 3.1.* Self-assessment rubric.

## Conclusion

This discussion of the NCTE *Beliefs About the Teaching of Writing* highlights the value of and rich possibilities for a greater focus on writing within the senior capstone course. Faculty without a background in writing instruction may feel overwhelmed by the prospect of adopting some of these suggested practices; therefore, the following chapters highlight specific strategies and assignments to make the increased incorporation of writing in the senior capstone less daunting.

# Part II

Writing Activities for
the Senior Capstone

# Chapter 4

Informal Writing: Promoting
Creativity and Critical Thinking

In senior capstones, instructors can use informal, brief writing assignments and activities to help students integrate new information, explore ideas, consider multiple perspectives, or practice specific critical-thinking skills. Informal writing activities may serve multiple purposes in the thinking and composing processes. For example, instructors can design informal writing assignments that help students invent, or generate, ideas for longer, more formal texts. Sitler (1993) called these "thought-gathering" (p. 23) activities. Hiemstra (2001) highlighted the value of journals in providing opportunities for reflection on "dilemmas, contradictions, and evolving worldviews" (p. 20). As such, journals and other informal writing activities support a number of outcomes important for the learning and development of college seniors, including reflection, critical thinking, and problem solving (Hiemstra, 2001). Moreover, students who engage in journaling learn to trust their inner voices (Hiemstra, 2001)—a factor Baxter Magolda (2001) suggested is central to the development of self-authorship. This chapter discusses strategies for incorporating two types of informal writing—freewriting and journaling—into the senior capstone.

## Freewriting and the Development of Critical Thinking

As one form of informal writing, freewriting (Elbow, 1998) can help make the classroom a workplace—a community of thinkers and creators, serious about developing and exchanging ideas. Usually written quickly for very brief periods of time and with "don't stop" as the primary instruction, freewriting can help students identify and consider ideas connected to class material without worrying about correctness, organization, or coherence. In fact, freewriting can lead to unexpected insights and help deepen analysis and understanding by creating a space for genuine exploration of ideas or concepts that may seem unfocused and unfamiliar (Hammond, 1991). In the senior capstone, instructors can ask students to freewrite about controversial or ambiguous issues that require in-depth consideration from multiple perspectives and then have them discuss their ideas in small groups to uncover new and richer ways of thinking about the topic. Because students have had an opportunity to generate ideas before the discussion, they are more likely to be engaged listeners and participants in the conversation that follows. In addition to using freewriting as preparation for discussion, students could

- think about an earlier learning experience, describing the strategies the worked well and considering how those strategies might be applied to the current learning context;
- review and evaluate ideas from the previous class that bothered or confused them;
- reflect on and synthesize class discussions, focusing on connecting arguments to the use of evidence; and
- summarize and comment on new ideas presented in the day's class.

Freewriting about what they learned in a specific class period will help students focus on the ideas most important to them and create a record of their new knowledge for further consideration. Bressoud (1999) used this strategy in math courses to uncover the range of student perceptions and to ensure students were honing in on central ideas of the course. He found this practice also helped students increase the specificity of their observations, an important mathematical analysis skill. In another example taken from an interdisciplinary seminar on women composers at IUP, students were expected to build a cross-disciplinary understanding of gender bias. To help them develop this insight, the instructor had students freewrite in response to prompts, such as this altered quotation from Samuel Johnson, identifying assumptions they have observed or experienced about what women cannot or should not do: "Sir, a woman preaching [or composing music, or other activity] is like a dog walking on his hind legs. It is not done well, but you are surprised to see it done at all" (S. Wheatley, personal communication, January 15, 2011). The discussion that followed built connections across disciplines as students considered the broader historical, cultural, and social contexts for the composer's life and career. Figure 4.1 offers suggestions for freewriting prompts.

**Prompts to reflect on prior class discussions**

- What ideas do you most remember from the discussion in our last class meeting?
- What would you like to see us discuss in greater depth today and why?

**Prompts to integrate knowledge at the end of class**

- What was the most important thing you learned today?
- Why was this knowledge valuable to you?
- Describe ways in which this new information challenges your current beliefs.
- What kind of research could you do to learn more about these new perspectives?

*Figure 4.1.* Sample freewriting prompts.

## *Facilitating an Appreciation for Multiple Perspectives*

Freewriting provides a powerful platform for students to reflect on their own learning experiences, but it also can be the basis for collaborative learning. Reading freewriting aloud in a small group helps students see that "completely unplanned, unstudied writing is often worth sharing" and hear "the pleasure of getting more voice in writing" (Elbow, 1991, p. 198). Perhaps more important, it can expose students to a variety of perspectives. Learning to value and critically evaluate diverse perspectives is an important prerequisite to critical thinking.

While freewriting prompts are typically loosely structured, more directive approaches can be used to encourage the development of particular patterns of thinking. For example, asking students to analyze and synthesize disciplinary concepts can help them integrate new knowledge with past learning experiences while developing higher level reasoning skills. In a senior seminar on the Culture of National Parks at IUP, students explored controversial ideas presented in the film *In the Light of Reverence* (McLeod & Maynor, 2001), a documentary about the development and recreational use of mountains and land formations sacred to Native Americans. The film illuminates different perspectives on the ways in which spirituality and religion create conflict among those who value the specific locations, such as Devils Tower, a national monument in the National Parks System. Students freewrote before and after small-group and whole-class discussions and focused the second freewrite on recommending changes to the National Parks Service Climbing Management Plan for Devils Tower (Figure 4.2).

- Freewrite for 15 minutes in response to the film *In Light of Reverence*. Choose two of the questions below to help you evaluate the information, interviews, and opinions revealed in this film.

  o What did you learn about the history of the Black Hills that was new to you?

  o How does this information change your view of land protection and ownership?

  o What biases are revealed through the interviews?

  o What perspectives from the climbing outfitters and ranchers were new to you?

  o What ideas from the Native Americans were surprising to you?

  o What does it mean to Native Americans to take care of, protect, and pray for land that is sacred?

  o How do these perspectives affect your opinion of the National Park Service's (NPS) Climbing Management Plan for Devils Tower, which includes voluntarily refraining from climbing this monolith during the most sacred month of June?

- After freewriting, discuss your ideas in small groups. One person should take notes of key points during your discussion. Together, agree on a summary of the group's ideas, and then prepare a list of recommendations for adjusting the NPS Management Plan. One group member will then report on your ideas to the class.

- Freewriting following whole-class discussion. Summarize and pull together (synthesize) the class's ideas for recommendations to changes to the NPS Climbing Management Plan. Comment on how this film changes your understanding of sacred spaces.

*Figure 4.2.* Freewriting prompts to develop respect for diverse perspectives.

## Journals: Integrating Personal Experience With Disciplinary Thinking

Journal writing can help students make connections between personal experiences and new ideas emerging from course material. Hiemstra (2001) described a number of journal types that could support reflection and the integration of personal experience, prior learning opportunities, and content within and across disciplines. The most appropriate for the senior capstone are presented below.

- *Learning journals* record student "thoughts, reflections, feelings, personal opinions, and even hopes or fears during an educational experience" (Hiemstra, 2001, p. 20). Entries might reflect responses to readings, course assignments, or classroom discussions. Learning journals can support students' career development and facilitate their connection to a discipline or field, especially when they capture students' "systematic observations of insights, events, and changes in personal perspectives during the course" (Hiemstra, 2001, p. 21). For example, in the senior seminar on women composers mentioned above, students integrated their personal experiences of listening to music with responses to course lectures and readings in a journal (S. Wheatley, personal communication, January 15, 2011). They also used their journals to write about their experiences developing the new skill of listening critically to music, which they then discussed in small groups.

- *Professional journals* allow students to document their professional growth and development and may provide a foundation for professional philosophy statements. A double-entry format may be useful in professional journals, with students reporting a narrative of meaningful field experiences in the left-hand column and using the right-hand column to record thoughts, feelings, ideas, and concerns about the field experience; "new learning, questions, and insights gained"; "a critique of the learning situation"; and "suggestions for future learning implications in the clinical context" (Gillis, 2001, p. 54).

Dunlap (2005) developed a capstone course for computer science majors in software engineering at the University of Colorado that used guided journal entries to help students reflect on software development problems. The prompts for the journal writing were designed to encourage students to comment on their confidence in software development, including questions such as

> What did you learn about your ability to work as a software development professional (analyst, designer, programmer, project manager) over the last three weeks? Are you confident that you can deal with the demands of real software projects? Why or why not? (Dunlap, p. 73).

The professional journal entries revealed that students increased their self-confidence as problem solvers in their profession as well as their sense of accomplishment as they applied theory to practice, which Dunlap noted would contribute to their success in the workplace.

- **_Interactive reading logs_** offer students a space to react to any elements in the course readings that they found "particularly meaningful or provocative" (Hiemstra, 2001, p. 23). Hiemstra (2001) encouraged students to use the log as a space for "simulated conversations with authors" to prompt "clarification or new insight" (p. 23). Such journals might be particularly powerful for students involved in simultaneous internship, practica, or service experiences, as it provides a space for them to reflect on the course reading in light of their field experiences.

  In a senior seminar on Appalachian culture at IUP, the instructor used structured reading responses to develop critical reading and writing skills, providing prompts asking students to attend to objective details and their personal responses (J. Cahalan, personal communication, January 21, 2013). For example, when reading historical sources, students paid attention to how the author integrated information from politics, economics, music, geography, and literature, and in particular, material from their major, and when writing in response to a novel, the class looked for historical information (J. Cahalan, personal communication, Feb. 7, 2013). These journal responses also helped students choose topics for their major research and presentation project and became part of the final portfolio for the course.

- **_Theory logs_** are similar to reading logs. Here, students record "what they perceive to be theoretical concepts, salient points, truths, bridges to known theory, ideas to be tested, and gaps in knowledge" while asking critical "questions about what they've read" (Hiemstra, 2001, p. 23). A theory log might be particularly useful in a capstone designed to help students synthesize knowledge across the major. Such reflections might form the basis of the kind of critical analysis of a discipline described by Baker (1997).

- **_Dialogue journals_** can be shared between students and instructors and may be particularly useful during internships or practica experiences. For example, student teachers can use a journal to record their successes, frustrations, and questions, while supervising faculty members provide feedback and help students discover solutions to teaching dilemmas (L. McPherson, personal communication, January 23, 2011). In this way, dialogue journals facilitate mentoring relationships. Fenwick (2001) also noted the value of using journal entries as a springboard for small-group discussions, commenting

> Seemingly, learners do not perceive the same closed authority of the text in each other's journal writing that they sometimes attribute to articles and books comprising the course reading list. They often respond to another's journal opinion by respecting, building on, probing, and questioning to inquire and then to challenge. (p. 38)

Journals of all kinds might be kept in simple notebooks, but many students embrace electronic journal formats because of their comfort with technology. Electronic journaling has several advantages. Provisional ideas recorded in the journal can be easily edited, expanded, and transferred to more formal writing assignments. When journals make use of social media (e.g., blogs), instructors and peers can read and comment on the student's developing ideas, enhancing his or her knowledge and understanding (Hiemstra, 2001).

## Other Opportunities for Informal Writing

To provide faculty with instructional resources for incorporating writing into disciplinary courses, Young (2011) compiled a collection of *small genres*. These brief, frequently informal writing assignments provide opportunities for synthesis, reflection, application, and assessment of learning experiences. For example, in an assignment appropriate for a range of courses requiring students to engage in data analysis, "The instructor will present various sets of experimental data. The student will describe the type of statistical test which best validates each data set and give reasons why that particular test was chosen" (Young, 2011, p. 16). The small genres frequently make use of or draw on workplace documents, offering ideas for writing activities in business, science, math, literary studies, popular culture, economics, and sports management. Young's collection included writing letters about research topics; exploring on-the-job scenarios; imagining alternate realities in which a problem is solved in a specific way; creating interview and survey questions; writing reviews and reports of relevant movies, television shows, or websites; responding to a class discussion; or summarizing a class activity, such as role-playing a solution to a problem.

## Evaluation of Informal Writing

By its very nature, informal writing promotes provisional thinking. As such, it may be counterproductive to assign grades to freewriting or journal responses. English (2001) noted,

> The fact that an instructor will read the journal may inhibit some learners from writing what is on their minds or from engaging in meaningful writing, reflecting, and learning. Consequently, the depth of the learning that is possible is often impeded. (p. 30)

Yet, the instructor's response to at least some portion of students' informal writing can be a valuable form of mentoring and help students "clarify the strengths in their current thinking" and promote "further investigation" (Hammond, 1991, p. 89). Especially when informal writing is a launching point for formal writing assignments in the course, students will appreciate a general but nonjudgmental response to the effectiveness of their efforts. Feedback might respond to

> overall fluency (thoroughness and variety of topics addressed), evidence of thoughtful reflection exploring various required issues or readings in the course, evidence of connection making, ... evidence of growth (perhaps incorporating earlier responsive suggestions), and evidence of critical thinking and questioning. (Fenwick & Parsons, 2000, cited in Fenwick, 2001, p. 44)

In addition, reviewing course journals can also improve the instructor's teaching effectiveness (Frantz, 1999).

Besides providing ungraded feedback, another evaluation alternative is to count the journals as class presentation. White (1999) used this approach at Harvey Mudd College with his math students, who engaged in journal writing to think about mathematical experiences in and out of class, approach problem solving more openly and deeply, and construct personal meaning about mathematics through reflection and conversation. By dialoguing with students in their journals, White felt this method encouraged them to speak more confidently in class and promoted intellectual growth in the discipline.

## Conclusion

Instructors in senior capstones have a variety of ways to use informal writing to nurture students' intellectual, personal, and social identities, as well as encourage reflection, synthesis, and the mutual construction of knowledge within a classroom community. Informal writing also helps students find their own voice: they write for its own sake, developing what Yagelski (2009) identified as a "way of being in the world" (2009, p. 7).

# Chapter 5

## Portfolios and Assessment of the Senior Capstone

A recent survey of employers (Hart Research Associates, 2013) found that 83% of respondents indicated that having an electronic portfolio of students' accomplishments, in addition to a résumé and course transcript, would help them better assess whether applicants had the skills and knowledge needed to succeed within their organization. While the portfolio's popularity as an assessment method appears to be growing elsewhere in higher education, it does not appear to be a particularly prevalent part of senior capstones. Henscheid (2000) reported that 37% of respondents to a national study incorporated portfolio development in the senior seminar, but a more recent study (Padgett & Kilgo, 2012) found that not quite a quarter (23.1%) of respondents included a portfolio as an end product of the senior capstone course. Though perhaps not reflected in current practice, the portfolio can be a particularly promising method for assessing individual learning and development as well as examining the effectiveness of a course, major program of study, or the undergraduate curriculum in meeting stated learning outcomes. This chapter addresses the benefits of portfolios, discusses strategies for developing portfolio assignments in the senior capstone, and describes strategies for using the portfolio as an assessment tool.

### The Portfolio: Benefits and Challenges

As seems evident from low rates of adoption of portfolios in senior capstones, some resistance to their use exists. For example, faculty may be reluctant to adopt portfolio grading for fear that it will increase their workload. Others may worry their judgment will be questioned in collective evaluation settings in which portfolios include samples of graded student work (Palomba & Banta, 1999). Portfolios also may appear unwieldy as a program assessment method because of the expense involved in collecting and archiving them—especially if they are not available electronically—and in training faculty to serve as evaluators. Yet, without such training (and even sometimes with it), questions related to the reliability and validity of portfolio evaluation persist (Palomba & Banta, 1999).

Despite these concerns, portfolios can be extremely valuable both as an assessment tool and as a vehicle for student learning. As Palomba and Banta (1999) noted, portfolio development demands that students "undertake complex work, providing an opportunity for teachers to challenge [them]" (p. 146). And students seem particularly receptive to this type of challenge, as this comment from a sophomore business communications major at Ball State University suggests:

> This class provided an opportunity for me to think about an important skill required in my career. For the first time in my life, I began to see the value of my assignments and how they connected to my future. I wish more teachers would require portfolios. (Jones, 1996, p. 287)

Both students and faculty value portfolios for their relevance to the curriculum and larger program objectives—something they do not always see with other program assessments. For example, because the portfolio derives from materials students are developing or have already developed for their courses, they may be more motivated to participate in the assessment. That the portfolio can also be used to support a future job search provides additional motivation for students to do their best work (Palomba & Banta, 1999). From a faculty perspective, demands for program assessment are frequently seen "as intrusive and irrelevant to the teaching-learning process. ... Because portfolios contain materials that have been generated by students as they progress through their programs, faculty see portfolios as linked to programmatic learning objectives" (Palomba & Banta, 1999, p. 146).

Creating a portfolio helps students "better understand how they learn and, thus, possibly become more responsible for their own learning and development" (Bresciani, Zelna, & Anderson, 2004, p. 77). When students have more choice and control over the work—as with portfolios—they are more likely to achieve autonomy. This approach supports integrative learning, as well. Faculty also experience unique learning opportunities when they participate in portfolio grading. Allen (2006) noted, "Faculty who review portfolios develop insights about student learning, and they also have a window into other instructors' courses and assignments, and expectations" (p. 163). These insights can form the basis of important discussions about how to align program or institutional learning objectives with educational experiences offered to students. Huyett (1996) suggested conversations about how portfolios are being used also help alleviate concerns about their adoption:

> Having our staff share with each other their strategies for making the portfolio useful gave them a sense of empowerment and a sense that what they do in their classrooms matters to others. This activity helped to take away the mystery as well as anxiety for those who wanted to use portfolios, but had been afraid to try. (p. 307)

## Defining the Portfolio

Portfolios are collections of student-generated artifacts that document learning and development (Bresciani et al., 2004; Palomba & Banta, 1999). Two basic types of portfolios exist. The first—variously called learning portfolios, process portfolios, or developmental portfolios—are "designed to document student growth" (Allen, 2006, p. 161) and to provide insight into how students learn (Reynolds & Rice, 2006). According to Reynolds and Rice (2006), learning portfolios "invite students to collect or create artifacts—essays, photographs, charts, letters, notes, and so on—that best represent their experience and engagement with the learning process in a particular subject area" (p. 2). As such, this kind of portfolio may not be evaluated for a grade.

A second, and perhaps more common, type of portfolio focuses on demonstrating "achievements, abilities, or talents" (Reynolds & Rice, 2006, p. 3) for assessment purposes. For this reason, it may be called an evaluation, presentation, or showcase portfolio. Closely related to the showcase portfolio is the professional portfolio, which collects artifacts to support job placement (Palomba & Banta, 1999).

Within the senior capstone, the type of portfolio students are asked to create may reflect the primary goals and concerns of the course. For example, if an overriding goal of the capstone is a focus on synthesizing and integrating concepts learned within the major or across the undergraduate experience, students might be asked to collect, and possibly revise, documents from a range of coursework. In other seminars, helping students learn the research process is an important goal. Here, the research portfolio (a type of learning portfolio described in more detail in chapter 6) may be as important a final product for the seminar as the research paper or presentation. Finally, if the capstone seeks to support career development, then a professional portfolio that includes select examples of student work along with an application dossier, values clarification and goal-setting activities, and reflections on themselves as developing professionals becomes an important process and product of the course.

However portfolios are designed, Reynolds and Rice (2006) suggested they have three common characteristics. First, a fundamental aspect of the portfolio is that students have a choice of what to include and how to present it. As they noted, "Telling portfolio keepers what to include, where, and in what form limits their learning" (p. 8)—thus, undermining one of the central reasons for adopting portfolios. Second, portfolios should encourage the inclusion of a variety of artifacts—"pieces of different lengths, written for different purposes and at different points in a writer's experience" (p. 8). The variety of pieces contained in the portfolio makes it a more valid measure of student learning and achievement than a single paper or exam, which only captures performance at a particular moment. Finally, the portfolio must offer the occasion for significant reflection or self-assessment. Such a reflective component allows students to look carefully at their "own patterns, strengths, and preferences" (p. 8) for managing discipline-specific tasks, learning new skills, or applying what has been learned in authentic situations.

### Components of the Portfolio

Bresciani et al. (2004) provided educators with a list of questions to ask when developing a portfolio assessment, two of which may offer guidance on the kinds of artifacts to have students incorporate in the portfolio: (a) "What is the primary purpose of the portfolio? To evaluate learning in a program or to promote and support individual student learning directly? [and (b)] What are the intended learning outcomes the portfolio will evaluate?" (p. 77).

If the portfolio is a vehicle for assessing learning outcomes within a major or across the undergraduate experience, individual faculty members may have limited flexibility in what they request from students. However, if the portfolio is designed primarily to document student performance within a single course, instructors have greater leeway in designing the portfolio assignment and guiding students in its development.

Ultimately, the items included in the portfolio should reflect the purpose for which it is being developed. For example, "photojournalism majors might be asked to include in their portfolios specific kinds of photographs that will be expected when they participate in job interviews" (Palomba & Banta, 1999, p. 135). Similarly, the School of Education at Samford University

(Box & Dean, 1995) engaged in a senior portfolio design project that not only served as a learning assessment but also as a tool for presenting students in the job market. The portfolio had three sections focused on professional information, curriculum planning, and instructional implementation and could include the following artifacts:

### Professional information

- résumé,
- evidence of teaching related experiences,
- awards and membership in professional organization, and/or
- statement of teaching philosophy.

### Curriculum planning

- teaching units developed in courses throughout the major, and/or
- model lesson plans with observational notes, if implemented.

### Instructional implementation

- photos, drawings, diagrams, or descriptions of classroom activities;
- bulletin boards designed and implemented in the classroom;
- worksheets, activities, or games developed by the student;
- journal of student teaching experience;
- summaries of conferences with cooperating teachers or supervising faculty; and/or
- evidence of assessment of student learning outcomes.

In other portfolio models, students may opt to include samples of work that have personal meaning, that showcase their development as an undergraduate, or that reflect something else they would like to demonstrate about their university experience, such as

- a collection of documents surrounding a major research project;
- fields notes of off-campus visits to conduct research;
- journal entries or reports on internships, practica, and service-learning experiences;

- career-exploration projects that include employment application documents (e.g., cover letters, résumés, or personal statements); and

- a collection of workplace documents relevant to the discipline (e.g., reports, letters, memos, or proposals).

If the portfolio is designed to be a showcase or presentation portfolio, students might include only final, revised versions of their work. For portfolios designed to demonstrate learning and development, students could be encouraged to provide a greater range of artifacts, including work considered weak or underdeveloped. Palomba and Banta (1999) noted that variety in terms of performance level allowed students "to contrast their best work with weaker work indicating how their best work distinguishes itself" and to demonstrate "their progress or how their thinking has changed about a subject" (p. 137).

## As a Vehicle for Reflection

As noted above, reflection is a primary characteristic of portfolio assessment. Regardless of the other components, students should be asked to provide a cover letter or essay describing the artifacts included and why those artifacts demonstrate the learning outcomes the portfolio is designed to assess. Reflective writing about educational experiences contributes to students' learning and development and also can reveal much about students' perspectives, making it useful in program-level assessments. A final cover letter for the portfolio also will help bring closure to a project, major course of study, or the entire undergraduate program of study. Instructors can design prompts for this letter that fit the discipline or subject matter of the course, as well make the prompts useful for larger assessment programs. Suskie (2004) offered a list of questions that students might address in such a cover letter:

- Which item represents your best work? Why?

- Which item is your most important work? Why?

- Which item is your most satisfying work? Why?

- Which item is your most unsatisfying work? Why?

- In which item did you stretch yourself the most, taking the greatest risk in exploring new territory? and

- List three things you learned by completing the portfolio. (quoted in Allen, 2006, pp. 161-162)

Figure 5.1 offers sample guidelines for a cover letter, describing a student's development as a writer, which may be appropriate in courses designed to help students develop disciplinary communication skills. The reflection could also be structured as a short essay or report with headings.

Reflecting on capstone projects does not have to be limited to considerations about the writing process; rather, it can be part of the evaluation of a range of learning outcomes. For example, Portland State University used a common assignment, a brief reflective essay tying course experiences to a program goal, as part of their assessment program (Rhodes & Agre-Kippenhan, 2004). In this essay, students addressed the ways they gained experience in one of the University Studies goals, choosing from communication, critical thinking, social and ethical responsibility, or human experiences. Students incorporated specific examples from their service-learning project, class discussions, course readings,

---

**Introduction**
- Begin the letter by introducing yourself to the reader (e.g., instructor, a review committee, or a future employer) and the subject, purpose, and organization of your portfolio.
- Explain how the portfolio is a response to an assignment in a course.
- Identify the major elements of the portfolio that will be described in greater detail in the letter.

**Discussion**
- In several paragraphs, describe and comment on the various documents in the portfolio, highlighting the ways in which these materials illustrate your development as a writer and expert in your discipline.
- Choose several passages in specific documents to consider in depth, explaining how you made particular rhetorical choices for improving your thesis, organization, development, or clarity.
- Discuss how you made these choices. What ideas for revising your work came from peer review, from conferences with your instructor, or from your own reading?

**Conclusion**
- Comment on how the portfolio represents your ways of thinking about its subject. How might you use this portfolio in your future? How might any of these documents be models for you in the future? What do you think you will need to learn as you continue to develop as a writer after graduation?

---

*Figure 5.1.* Guidelines for a portfolio cover letter about writing development.

or individual projects. Faculty designed rubrics to review students' essays, and the results, although very positive, helped them align course goals and program assessment more tightly (Rhodes & Agre-Kippenhan, 2004).

The department of mathematics at Kutztown University of Pennsylvania found portfolios, and especially the reflective essay, extremely helpful in assessing disciplinary learning outcomes. The department required all majors to take a senior seminar in which they created a portfolio of artifacts from any math courses that described and recorded their growth during the major. The essay explained the underlying unity in all the documents the student chose to put into his or her portfolio (Frantz, 1999).

Students will develop a deeper understanding of how they made connections with the subject matter as they describe their selections and explain the ways in which their documents demonstrate the achievement of specific course, program, or institutional goals. As they direct their readers to notice rhetorical choices, writers also explain the rationale for these choices, linking the specific passage to the overall purpose of the portfolio. If the portfolio will be used for program-level assessment, students might also be asked to reflect on how their portfolio selections illustrate learning from other courses and demonstrate the integration of knowledge from multiple areas—the major, liberal arts coursework, and cocurricular experiences. To conclude the reflection, students can consider how they expect to apply their new knowledge and understanding to the next phase of their lives.

## Portfolio Development

Students need a clear orientation to the instructor's expectations for portfolio development. The following guidelines can help instructors determine the scope of the portfolio and communicate its parameters to students:

- Provide a planning document for exploring the subject, purpose, audience, organization, and scope of the portfolio. Such a planning document should address these questions:

  ○ What is the overall purpose of the portfolio?

  ○ Who will read the portfolio?

  ○ How will the writer or others use the portfolio?

  ○ What is the subject of the portfolio?

- ○ What are the required components?
- ○ What are the expectations for the overall length of the portfolio or the number of different documents in the portfolio?
- ○ How will the portfolio be organized?
- ○ What are the expectations for the style of writing in the portfolio?
- ○ What components must students design?
- ○ What are possible genre or format choices for portfolio selections?
- ○ What graphics or tables might be relevant?
- ○ What possibilities are there for incorporating nonprint media (e.g., sound or visual media)?
- ○ Is an electronic portfolio an option? If so, how will it be developed and implemented?
- ○ What is the timeline for the portfolio?
- Stress that students will make decisions about what goes into the portfolio.
- Emphasize that students will make selections for the final collection that demonstrate specific learning goals (e.g., integrating their learning, showcasing disciplinary understanding, illustrating various perspectives on a topic).
- Clarify how and when the portfolio will be evaluated and graded.

Because portfolio assessment holds evaluation until the end, students may feel anxious about their performance. Regular feedback from the instructor and/ or peers on various components of the portfolio may allay some of these concerns, while ensuring that students produce a more robust collection of artifacts. A regular schedule of progress report deadlines can also help students stay on track. The first report might ask students to create their own plan for their portfolio and write a memo to the instructor explaining their choices. Instructors may review this memo and use it during conferences with a small group of students. Or, the instructor can write a memo or brief e-mail in response to the student. For a developmental portfolio, such a memo may become part of the final portfolio. It might also be useful in writing the reflective essay. Later in the process, students may write a progress memo describing their revision plans or the kinds of support they plan to seek (e.g., working with a tutor at the writing center) to develop the portfolio. Finally, students could report on the success of those revisions, based on feedback from peers or others.

Regular progress reports can be particularly effective when coupled with peer review activities because, in addition to describing what they have done, students actually have to produce some work to share in their small groups. The focus of peer review will depend on the document(s) being reviewed and where students are in the writing process (e.g., early draft, revised draft). For a full portfolio review, students should prepare a complete document, with the exception of the final cover letter, in which they have purposefully arranged their selections.

### Electronic Portfolios

Portfolios frequently are collections of printed materials, but as the definition of literacy expands, so too do the kinds of texts students are likely to produce. Electronic portfolios (i.e., e-portfolios) may be a more appropriate venue for students who develop videos, computer programs, applications, or websites; compose music; catalog live performances; or collect photographs or other visual media. Reynolds and Rice (2006) noted that e-portfolios are also easier to archive and maintain. A taskforce for the Conference on College Composition and Communication (CCCC, 2007) identified other advantages, such as helping students to

- synthesize diverse evidence and ideas;
- link artifacts from many courses;
- enhance reflection as a critical-thinking skill;
- learn more about writing for an authentic audience in the digital realm;
- understand that writing is dynamic and evolving;
- develop and manage a virtual identity, including how written documents represent their identities, especially their professional ethos or characteristics; and
- articulate how they have been meeting their own learning goals.

Despite these many benefits, instructors may be reluctant to incorporate e-portfolios unless they have adequate support services for the technological components, as well as for faculty development in digital instruction. E-portfolios, especially those that students begin in their first year and continue through their capstone courses, require a substantial financial and instructional commitment from institutions. Yet, given that they require students to develop familiarity and comfort in the digital realm and encourage integrative and reflective thinking, e-portfolios can enhance learning in many ways and help students develop additional electronic communication skills.

## Evaluating the Portfolio

Portfolios can be used to assess student achievement at the individual course level, but they also can provide insight into how well departmental or institutional learning objectives are being achieved or the kinds of experiences students have and find most salient during their undergraduate careers. Culminating projects, especially portfolios from a senior capstone, are ideal for program-level assessments because they provide a complete context within which to view student development (AAC&U, 2004) and can help institutions articulate definitions of good writing (Moore, O'Neill, & Huot, 2009). This section explores both levels of portfolio assessment.

### Course-Level Assessments

Reynolds and Rice (2006) noted responding to portfolios need not be time consuming, assuming that students have received regular feedback on the artifacts included. Brief conferences and e-mail responses to progress reports will help students understand what they need to do to meet their goals. If students are using artifacts from other courses rather than creating new materials in the seminar, Allen (2006) suggested portfolio evaluation can be "based on the quality of the reflective essay, organization, and conformity to formatting requirements" (p. 164). She added that such an approach "rewards student effort and encourages them to reflect on their own academic and personal development" (Allen, p. 164). Because grading is reduced in a portfolio process, instructors increase their roles as respondents, giving more authority to students (Huot, 2002).

Both instructors and students benefit from a clear understanding of how portfolios will be evaluated at the outset of their development. At its most basic, portfolio evaluation might involve a simple checklist, indicating whether all the required elements are present. This evaluation might be appropriate for learning or developmental portfolios. In other cases, "student portfolios are evaluated on the appropriateness and quality of items they contain" (Palomba & Banta, 1999, p. 139). Reynolds and Rice (2006) offered a series of questions to guide the development of a scoring guide:

- Do the reflective elements provide reasons for students' choices and identify the changes they have made to essays or projects in preparing the portfolio?

- Are the entries focused, developed, organized, or do they reflect the qualities of good writing your course has emphasized?

- Are the arrangement and/or navigational scheme effective?

- How much revision is enough?

- How much should the writing process count?

- How much should improvement count?

- How do I account for variety? and

- What am I looking for? (pp. 49-50)

While Reynolds and Rice (2006) focused primarily on the writing process, instructors will want to consider the learning outcomes most appropriate for their discipline and course and determine how they might be best be showcased in the portfolio. Figure 5.2 provides an example of a scoring guide for a business communications portfolio.

In some cases, students are required to present or defend their portfolio formally before an audience that may include a panel of faculty members, their peers, and/or external evaluators. For example, business majors at Rappahannock Community College compiled portfolios that included a culminating project, résumé, job application, and cover letter in response to a particular job advertisement (Smith & Crowther, 1996). Their portfolios were evaluated by a citizen's advisory committee, which "returns direct and applicable comments on the professional quality of the students' projects" (Smith & Crowther, 1996, p. 116). The feedback students received also allowed them to revise job application materials for greater placement success.

While the evaluation process is a valuable learning experience for the student who compiled the portfolio, it might also be an important processing tool for his or her peers. Portfolio presentations can be integrated into a final synthesizing class activity during which students conduct roundtable discussions, with each student contributing ideas about what they learned and how it is meaningful to them.

**Your portfolio can earn a potential of 45 points.**
**These points are allocated as follows:**

**Organization (15 points)**

| | | | | | |
|---|---|---|---|---|---|
| Presentation is logical. | 1 | 2 | 3 | 4 | 5 |
| Reflection statement and selected artifacts are coordinated. | 1 | 2 | 3 | 4 | 5 |
| Coherence is apparent. | 1 | 2 | 3 | 4 | 5 |
| Total | | | | | _____ |

**Content (15 points)**

| | | | | | |
|---|---|---|---|---|---|
| Selection of items included is appropriate. | 1 | 2 | 3 | 4 | 5 |
| Examples demonstrate overall communication ability. | 1 | 2 | 3 | 4 | 5 |
| Examples effectively support specific ability identified. | 1 | 2 | 3 | 4 | 5 |
| Total | | | | | _____ |

**Presentation (10 points)**

| | | | | | |
|---|---|---|---|---|---|
| Items are mechanically correct. | 1 | 2 | 3 | 4 | 5 |
| Appearance is professional. | 1 | 2 | 3 | 4 | 5 |
| Total | | | | | _____ |

**Overall Effect (5 points)**

| | | | | | |
|---|---|---|---|---|---|
| Impact on the evaluator | 1 | 2 | 3 | 4 | 5 |
| Total | | | | | _____ |

**Total Points Earned** _____

*Figure 5.2.* Scoring guide for business communications portfolio. Adapted from Linda Annis and Carollee Jones, Chapter 15, p. 188, in Seldin and Associates, *Improving College Teaching*, Boston, MA: Anker Publishing, 1995. Reprinted with permission.

## Program-Level Assessments

As noted throughout the chapter, portfolios in senior seminars may contain or be entirely created from projects students developed over the course of the undergraduate experience. In this case, students would choose selections; revise them if necessary; and write a reflective letter, essay, or preface about the selections, explaining how the selections illustrate particular elements of their educational journey. The experiences students are asked to highlight would be identified by a department or larger university program and related to learning outcomes (e.g., as analysis, synthesis, multicultural awareness, or interdisciplinary understanding) targeted by the educational institution.

The prospect of portfolio review at the program level may seem even more daunting than at the course level, but Palomba and Banta (1999) note, "It's not unusual to ask all students in a program to submit portfolios for decision making about individual progress, but to review only a sample for programmatic assessment" (p. 145). Review committee members can approach those portfolios selected for review in a number of ways. For example, after being trained, they might use a scoring guide or rubric designed to highlight programmatic areas of interest, or they may "answer a set of open-ended questions about programmatic strengths and weaknesses evidenced from student portfolios" (Palomba & Banta, p. 145).

Whether assessment is tied to portfolios, essays, reports, or other documents, the questions that we ask about student work should reflect the goals of the course, major, or program. In institution-wide assessment programs, a specially designated committee works to gather students' documents, determine the measures to be used, design assessment rubrics tailored specifically to the program of study, review findings, and prepare reports for distribution to administrators and faculty for discussion. Before implementing curricular changes in its Liberal Studies (LS) program, IUP undertook this process to study learning outcomes based on the categories of Informed Learners, Empowered Learners, and Responsible Learners. Over four years, the subcommittee created and revised a set of rubrics based on the general learning outcomes for all LS courses but tailored them specifically to meet criteria relevant for majors from each college. For example, Informed Learners were defined as students who "understand nature and society through forms of inquiry fundamental to the sciences, the humanities, and the arts. Learners are informed by knowledge and ways of knowing that extend beyond core concepts enabling them to link theory and practice" (McKee & Pistole, 2010, p. 11). For documents received from The College of Natural and Social Sciences, this category was evaluated according to two traits: (a) "understanding scientific or social scientific method" and (b) "awareness of the role of science or social science in society" (McKee & Pistole, 2010, p. 11).

Empowered Learners were defined as "critical thinkers who demonstrate intellectual agility and creativity and the ability to manage or create change," are able "to derive meaning from experience and observation," can "communicate well in diverse settings and employ various strategies to solve problems," and demonstrate a "mastery of intellectual and practical skills" (McKee & Pistole, 2010, p. 13). Two traits indicative of empowered learning were rated for all majors: (a) the "ability to argue or explain" and (b) "discrimination regarding quality of sources" (McKee & Pistole, 2010, p. 13).

Research on learning outcomes in senior seminars has identified growth in critical thinking through writing projects. In such research studies, faculty have designed assignments that help students demonstrate particular thinking skills, such as analysis or synthesis, and asked students to use vocabulary that connects writing tasks to the desired outcomes. For example, Hummer (1997) found that the capstone paper is an effective and efficient way to evaluate the development of critical thinking when specific assignment criteria are matched to learning goals, using verbs that reflect the desired skills, such as interpret, criticize, discriminate, summarize, and justify. At Southern Illinois University Edwardsville, the capstone course in psychology, a research-intensive experience, requires students to design and conduct an empirical research study and publicly present their findings. The department reviews these student projects each semester, with faculty working together to develop an assessment system to measure learning outcomes (Sullivan & Thomas, 2007). There may be challenges involved in designing, implementing, and carrying out program-level assessments with portfolios, but as Frantz notes, "The strengthening of the major that results is worth the effort" (1999, p. 34).

## Conclusion

Portfolios can serve multiple purposes in the senior capstone—helping students synthesize and integrate information and experiences, document their learning and development, and demonstrate mastery or achievement. In this way, they can support both course-level and programmatic assessment efforts. As such, portfolios provide valuable insight into the kinds of experiences students have within a major or the larger undergraduate curriculum and how they make sense of those experiences. Faculty gain a greater understanding of which experiences support (or in some cases fail to support) desired performance in the capstone course. While portfolios have yet to be widely adopted as an instructional strategy in the senior capstone, they hold great promise for supporting student learning and development and for assessing the undergraduate experience.

# Chapter 6

## Strategies for Supporting Research Writing

The academic research paper is likely the predominant writing assignment in the senior capstone. Two disciplinary surveys of capstone courses support this finding. For example, Hauhart and Grahe (2010) examined the organization of seminars in the social sciences and reported that 72% of the courses surveyed incorporated an extended paper with a literature review, 95% identified the research paper as a major course outcome, and 45% involved independent data collection. In a similar study of undergraduate research experiences in economics departments, McGoldrick (2008) found that nearly half of respondents (48.7%) offered a capstone course, and in 80% of those courses, students participated in specific research process activities. These experiences included developing a research question (62.7%), conducting a literature review (58.7%), locating and analyzing data (60%), drawing conclusions (65.3%), comparing conclusions to the literature (41.3%), and presenting research to peers (62.7%) and faculty (34.7%). Because students are likely to have limited exposure to and practice with these kinds of tasks earlier in their college careers, they may need support to perform them successfully in the senior capstone. This chapter examines a range of assignments that help students define a research problem and practice summarizing, synthesizing, and critiquing the literature as part of developing their own projects.

### Inherent Challenges in Producing the Research Paper

The Council of Writing Program Administrators (2011) defines rhetorical knowledge as "the ability to analyze and act on understandings of audiences, purposes, and contexts in creating and comprehending texts" (p. 6). Unfortunately, much of the writing students do in school—at the middle and high school level and into college—exists in a kind of rhetorical vacuum. Students most frequently write to their instructors with the purpose of demonstrating their mastery of specific content or writing conventions. They write according to templates, pre-scribed formats, or carefully scripted formulae. Previous instructors have told them what forms to use, how to organize their texts, what words or phrases to use or avoid, and how many pages they must write. Such instruction removes the challenge of analyzing, evaluating, and selecting genres or forms to respond to the needs of a specific audience for a particular purpose. Therefore, college seniors may be unfamiliar, uncomfortable, and inexperienced with making the kinds of choices the culminating research project in the senior capstone demands.

The independent research project is an ill-structured problem, requiring students to integrate new information, ideas, and theories. They are expected to come up with an original research question—one that explores an issue of immediate interest and value to a particular disciplinary or professional com-munity. Next, students must examine each aspect of the rhetorical problem—subject, audience, purpose—to answer a range of questions related to developing a text, such as

- How much space will I need to cover this topic?

- How familiar is my audience with my topic? How does their level of familiarity shape my decisions about overall length? Length of specific sections of the text?

- What aspects of this topic will my audience be most likely to value? What are the areas of potential controversy of which I need to be aware?

- What kind of evidence will my audience value?

- Why I am writing to this particular audience at this particular time? What do I hope to accomplish?

Such assignments increase opportunities for students to become more independent as thinkers and writers, to develop creativity and authority, and to own their work more fully. At the same time, students' epistemological develop-ment may play a role in the kinds of questions they ask about their topics and how they frame responses. In a review of the composition studies literature, Skipper (2009) found that cognitive complexity influences the ways students define the rhetorical demands of writing assignments. In other words, cogni-tive development may place limitations on students' ability to perform certain tasks—simply because they do not define them as an important aspect of the writing process. For example, more than half of the first-year writers whose typical level of functioning was pre-reflective thinking failed to identify other possible solutions in a policy essay, limiting their ability to evaluate the effectiveness of their proposal fully (Skipper, 2009). For many students engaged in independent research, defining an appropriately sophisticated rhetorical problem will be particularly challenging. As such, students may need support and practice in approaching the more developmentally complex tasks presented by the independent research project. Two strategies described below —the I-Search Process and the research portfolio—provide structures allowing students to explore their choices and practice expressing their ideas and arguments in varied forms. These strategies also help them apply rhetorical knowledge contextually and then choose the most effective focus, tone, style, organization, and information.

## The I-Search Process

Beyond cognitive readiness to identify complex research questions, students must have a personal commitment to them to develop effective arguments. As such, students should be able to explore topics of their own choosing. Beach and Doerr-Stevens (2009) recommended adopting a rhetoric of "significance and transformation" by encouraging students to explore what matters to them, gather evidence, and cite "personal, ethical, or moral reasons for why the status quo isn't working and needs to be addressed" (p. 462). Argumentation can then take on transformative power as students evaluate belief systems surrounding the problem and propose solutions (Beach & Doerr-Stevens, 2009). Danielewicz (2008) argued that students need to keep the *I* at the center of their expression so they can cultivate voice, identity, and authority, while they learn to craft the more public voice that is part of engaging with the discourse of their disciplines. The I-Search research process ensures student investment in the topic while providing a structure to help them cultivate more sophisticated questions about a topic.

Developed by Macrorie (1988), the I-Search process differs from traditional research papers in that it engages students in writing a first-person narrative describing their exploration of a question, the evolution of that question, and how what they learned is likely to shape their lives in the future (Assaf, Ash, Saunders, & Johnson, 2011). The crux of the I-Search paper is "the story of the search …, explaining the route taken to find information and answer important questions, recording the way the central question evolves and changes"

(Lyman, 2006, p. 62). Student reflection on personal learning is also key to this type of assignment, with students closing the paper by considering how they "might continue to investigate this question in the future" (Lyman, 2006, p. 62). In this way, an I-Search essay might serve as the reflective component in a portfolio developed in the senior capstone, as described in the previous chapter.

Yet, as Lyman (2006) notes, this type of assignment "emphasizes a sort of writing often banned from traditional research": a "first-person point of view" and "findings … presented … as the story of the search, not as objective, final truth" (p. 63). For this reason, faculty may question the value of the I-Search process in a senior capstone, especially if one goal of the course is to help students learn to emulate the scholarly practice of the discipline. In fact, Davis and Shadle (2000) have argued the personal essay with a foundation in the I-Search process should move toward a more intellectual and public product by directing students to consider how their personal interests are relevant to their readers. Such an expectation is probably typical for research projects in the senior capstone. Thus, a student whose personal search explores whether he or she should become a physician's assistant might transform this into a research question with broader public interest, such as What kinds of changes in health care are behind doctors turning care over to assistants?

Faculty who eschew the idea of the personal essay in the capstone might still use the I-Search process to help students structure an independent research project. For example, students could begin to form a research problem by reflecting on the following questions:

- What do I presently know about this topic?
- What are my beliefs and values relative to this topic?
- What experiences have I had that led me to be interested in this topic?
- What are some possible controversies within this topic?

In addition to guiding students through a research project, Klausman (2007) found that as students probed research on topics of personal concern, noting how others' arguments did not fit their experiences, they felt a greater sense of authority over the topic and were more ready to establish their own arguments. The questioning process also develops the critical perspective necessary to distinguish current knowledge from assumptions and gaps in information and ideas. Thus, students may more readily articulate the exigency for examining a particular issue or investigating a specific problem. Similarly, the I-Search process may help students identify, organize, and synthesize relevant material for a literature review. Early in the process, reflections on what has been learned might help students narrow or define a research question more clearly. Reflections later in the process provide students with insight into implications for future research and practice—a critical component of research essays in the sciences and social sciences.

If students are not writing formal I-Search essays, faculty may still elect to have them document their research process (e.g., research activities, findings, reflections) in a journal, using a two-column format. For example, as students formulate research questions, one column might describe what they know about the topic and the second what they would like to learn about it. Similarly, a two-column approach to a search of the literature might summarize a source in one column while reflecting on its usefulness for the current project, evaluating its methodology or analysis, or connecting it to other sources found in the second. The journal could serve as the basis for conferences with faculty or peer-review discussions.

Such a structure makes visible for students aspects of the research process that more seasoned researchers seem to know intuitively. Moreover, by constantly asking students to reflect on and raise new questions about their investigations, the I-Search process increases the likelihood that students will generate more compelling research questions and richer analyses of their results.

## The Research Portfolio

The *research portfolio* is a collection of diverse formats, genres, informal pieces, and revised work. As a learning portfolio (a type of portfolio discussed briefly in chapter 5), the research portfolio might include memos, FAQs (i.e., frequently asked questions), summaries, and critiques. Like the informal writing previously described, this collection of materials provides a forum for summary, speculation, hypothesis testing, and synthesis in response to a student's research question. The following list presents examples of writing assignments that might be used to help students develop a longer research project and, as such, might be included in the research portfolio:

*Workplace or technical writing artifacts*
- memos and letters informing peers and the instructor of topic choices, research questions, discoveries, and problems;

- progress updates and reports on research;

- summaries of scholarly articles;

- analyses of specific elements in scholarly articles, such as an author's use of current, credible, and authoritative information to support an argument;

- a synthesis of research;

- surveys relevant to research topics; and

- interview transcripts, reports, and analysis.

### Personal writing
- reflections on the research and learning processes, and

- experiences and observations relevant to the topic.

### Collaboratively written pieces about the research process and material
- plans for group presentations.

### Drafts for future revision
- research essays,

- critiques,

- individual or group presentation plans,

- newsletters (individually or collaboratively created), and

- web-based assignments (e.g., websites, multimedia and multimodal projects, FAQs, notes and guides to fine arts performances and exhibitions, blogs).

Because learning portfolios are primarily a vehicle for demonstrating growth or development, they frequently are not evaluated for a grade. For this reason, the research portfolio can be a safe space for students to explore and practice writing in the genres of their disciplines and/or local communities. Their work may begin by learning to analyze genre rhetorically, asking questions that interweave their academic, personal, and professional identities, such as Who uses this genre regularly and why? How am I like this or different? How does using this genre facilitate communication with my reader? and How does this genre represent my professional identity? Faculty can guide students in answering these questions through classroom discussion, small-group conversations, or informal writing assignments tied to readings in the course. As students discover for themselves what it means to be a member of a community that uses a particular genre, they can also notice the values associated with this membership and see how it fits their developing identities.

Additionally, in the research portfolio, students can learn to combine informative writing (e.g., a memo), which emphasizes writing to communicate, with expressive writing, highlighting personal reflection. Writing prompts that cause students to read for specific information and then report and comment on it combine transactional and expressive purposes in writing. For example, in an upper-level English course on teaching writing at the University of South Carolina, students wrote responses to 10 readings over the course of the semester. In particular, they were asked to

- summarize the piece, identifying central arguments and issues;

- identify one or two specific passages that interest you and comment on them. For example, did the passage surprise you? Teach you something you did not know? Strike you as illogical or poorly argued? Give you an idea that you would like to explore further? Contradict your beliefs or other reading you have done on the issue? Explain; and

- pose one or two substantive questions that can act as springboards for our class discussion of the reading, such as How does the piece add to or complicate our understanding of what it means to write or teach writing? What arguments invite closer analysis or criticism? and What arguments invite comparison to other work we've read? In short, about what issues in the text would you like to hear your classmates' insights?

While cast as a one-page essay, the assignment could easily be transformed into a memo addressed to their colleagues (i.e., classmates, instructor) designed to explore the contribution of individual readings to their understanding of writing instruction and to set an agenda for their work in the course. This type of structured response process will help students identify issues that especially interest them, leading into more formal research, writing, and communication tasks, including final oral presentations. Students can be encouraged to use this assignment as a model for how they read and respond to sources they review for their independent research projects.

The next section examines other possibilities for the research portfolio in greater detail. In addition to supporting the development of the capstone project, these particular writing activities offer students the opportunity to develop skills with applicability beyond the research paper and the senior seminar.

### Using Memos in the Research Portfolio

A 2004 report by the National Commission on Writing noted that business leaders identified three primary types of workplace documents: (a) memos and other correspondence, 70%, (b) formal reports, 62%, and (c) technical reports, 59%. Yet, students may have few opportunities to practice these genres. Short technical documents that record, report on, or evaluate the research process not only advance students' work on capstone projects but also encourage the development of professional and practical communication skills. A former mechanical engineering student at Texas A&M University found that writing weekly reports on his team's research and applications leading up to a final extensive report on their project prepared him very well for the collaborative research, writing, and presenting he did in graduate school and eventually in the workplace (C. Schneider, personal communication, September 3, 2012).

The informal but business-voice style of a memo, combined with its pre-scribed format, makes it ideal for communicating with the instructor and small, working groups of peers about ideas, plans, and concerns. Memos can help students explore ideas, plan research and drafts, seek clarification, engage in self-assessment, and document accomplishments for letters of recommendation. Writing memos about their research plans, findings, and questions also gives students practice in audience analysis, one of the skills Brent (2012) and his interns found crucial to successful writing in the workplace. When students have to identify a real reader in the *To* line, they can easily begin to analyze how their relationship with that individual influences their style, tone, voice, phrasing, and development. Because the genre of the memo assumes shared knowledge, experiences, and contexts, all of which influence word choice, phrasing, and depth of explanation, students must evaluate their degree of intimacy and familiarity with their reader and make choices that are appropriate and reasonable to sustain the relationship. For example, in the memo writing assignment in Figure 6.1, students may feel comfortable assuming a fairly informal tone in writing to their classmates, but they also will need to assess their group members' level of familiarity with their research topics to determine whether technical terms or theories need defining or explaining.

### The Research Critique

In many disciplines, being able to write an analytical critique of scholarly research is an important skill. For students completing an independent research project, a series of critiques can form the basis of a literature review. At a minimum, the practice of preparing critiques on course readings provides students

**Assignment:** Write reviews of research articles as memos.

*Overview:* The purpose of this activity is to help your group members become informed about your topic so that they can talk with you about your research and ideas and help you develop an awareness of a variety of perspectives on your topic.

*Task:* Write a memo in which you summarize and comment on one of the articles from your research.

- In the To line, list the names of your small-group members.

- In the Subject line, name the title of the article, its author, and the publication information.

- In the body of the memo, summarize the key points of the article in one paragraph.

- In another paragraph, comment on the most interesting information you found in the article. Integrate two quotations from the article that help demonstrate your opinions about interesting information or ideas.

- Conclude by identifying any questions or problems you have about this article. For example, does the writer's bias bother you in any way? What terms or explanations did the writer use that confused you? How might this writer's perspective appeal to an audience that has a different view than your own? How might his or her ideas and findings be useful to other students who are working on similar topics?

**Small-Group Discussion**

*Overview:* The purpose of your small-group meeting today is to read each other's summaries and discuss the information, ideas, and problems in the memos and gain new perspectives on your material. Each member should leave the discussion with at least one new idea or way of thinking about his or her topic.

*Process:*
- Exchange memos in a continuous loop so that you read the memos from all your group members. Make no comments while everyone is reading.

- Each person should take the floor and guide a discussion about his or her memo. Ask group members for their feedback on ideas, information, and problems.

After you have discussed all the memos, you should write a note at the bottom of your own memo about classmates' responses, describing at least one new way of thinking about the topic that you can pursue for additional research in published material, in interviews, or through Internet searches.

*Figure 6.1.* Memo forms supporting research.

with important tools for analyzing prior research that can help them refine their own research question, method, and conclusions. The critique is a demanding genre and requires complex reading, thinking, reviewing, and composing abilities. Often, it is limited to one or two pages and, thus, presents more composing challenges to students who will struggle to be concise yet thorough in their argumentation. Breaking this task down into separate critical-thinking components, sequencing the analytical tasks to build toward claims, and using clear categories or headings in a document will help students write more successful critiques. Instructors may find that demonstrating or modeling how they read an article and organize ideas and information to write a critique will be very helpful to students as they begin this process.

Brookfield (2011) recommended generating a set of questions that focus on an author's use of assumptions, evidence, and illustrations to sequence a critical analysis of a text (e.g., a scholarly article). To develop an overall argument about the quality of an article, instructors can ask students to write a few sentences in response to questions, such as

- What are the author's underlying assumptions? Respond to the validity and accuracy of these assumptions.

- What kinds of explanations seem inadequate?

- What contradictions or inconsistencies affect the author's credibility?

- What is the author's most convincing use of supporting evidence?

- How does the author use empirical evidence?

- How is the author influenced by his or her disciplinary philosophy or theory?

- How do the author's conclusions follow from his or her use of explanations?

- How does the author's use of illustrations affect his or her argument? What illustrations do you find convincing and credible?

Such questions help guide students' reading of a research article and may help them generate content for a critique. However, they also will need guidance on the best way to structure a critique. The following questions can help instructors create a reading, thinking, and writing process for the research critique assignment:

- What is the overall purpose of this critique? How can I communicate that to my students?

- What are the specific components of a critique in my discipline? How can I present these components to students so they can use them in their critiques? What information about each component do they need to know to complete each section successfully?

- What kinds of information do students need to read to build an analysis? How can I coach them to read in this way?

- How can I coach students on identifying their need for background information on a topic to complete a successful critique? What strategies will be most useful to them in finding that information?

- What kind of analytical statement do I expect them to develop about this article? How can I model this kind of statement for them?

- What should a finished critique look like? How can I model this for my students?

Figure 6.2 shows a sequence of geochemistry reading and writing tasks to develop students' ability to critique scholarly articles and, eventually, be able to respond as authorities to academic manuscripts submitted for peer review. An assessment rubric for evaluating this writing assignment is presented in Figure 6.3.

### Web-Based Writing Assignments

It is clear that literacy in the 21st century has moved beyond the ability to read and write traditional, print-based texts. Students must be equipped to consume critically and to produce a wide range of media, including digital texts, audio files, images, video, and others. As with using business documents to help students develop their own research projects, faculty in the senior capstone can include digital and/or multimodal compositions as part of the research portfolio. Creating in different media helps students develop valuable skills that can transfer beyond the capstone and a specific research project. Two web-based possibilities for inclusion in the research portfolio—the FAQ and blogs—are described in more detail below.

**Organic Geochemistry**

Writing assignment accompanying Grice et al. (2005). Photic zone euxinia during the Permian-Triassic superanoxic event. *Science, 307*(5710), 706-709. DOI: 10.1126/science.1104323

*Overview:* This writing assignment takes you through the steps to conduct a thorough evaluation of a scientific paper: (a) getting the gist of the paper, (b) determining its geologic and / or environmental context, (c) identifying the details of the technique, and (d) evaluating the science. Although researchers do all these steps at once, you will begin by doing parts of this process first for an in-class discussion. Following the discussion, you will combine what you have learned and write a one-two-page paper before the next class, synthesizing the information you and your classmates gathered and reflecting any conclusions you have drawn about the paper.

There are three parts to this assignment. Bring all work to class for discussion. As class starts, we will photocopy your text for your classmates' benefit for Part 2.

**Part 1 (about one-two paragraphs):**

As you read, make a list of the vocabulary with which you are unfamiliar. Write definitions for these terms. If there are terms for which you cannot find good definitions or about which you have questions, bring them to the class discussion.

Write a short paragraph identifying the uncertainty that this paper resolves. What aspect of paleoclimate was unknown that this paper attempts to address?

What is the major conclusion of the paper? Use one quotation to demonstrate the authors' concluding analysis.

**Part 2 (one-two paragraphs):**

In class you will be assigned one of the following tasks:

- Where and when in the geologic record is this work set? Report the geologic time down to the finest scale possible. Use the Internet to determine what the plate configuration was during the geologic time period in question. If you get stuck looking for paleoplate configurations, try Googling paleogeography or paleomaps. Capture an image from the web that shows paleoplate configurations during this time. Be sure you get an image of the relevant continent (e.g., if the study takes place in Asia, do not provide a paleomap of the Antarctic).

- What is the organic geochemical marker being used in this study? What is its structure, and what is its presumed function within biological systems? Do the authors indicate that diagenesis has any effects on its utility?

- What is the method being used to measure the marker? Describe in your own words the basic chemical concepts used to measure the marker in question. Are there any uncertainties associated with this technique? If so, do the authors address these uncertainties?

- What are Chlorobiaceae? Use the web and physical resources at the library to develop a useful, low-jargon description of these organisms. Include their food source (i.e., autotrophs or heterotrophs), their environmental restrictions (i.e., oxic or anoxic), and their locations in the modern world. Note any unusual aspects of their metabolism.

**Part 3:**

Write a one-two page summary of Grice et al., 2005. Include relevant material from items 1-4 above. Consider the stated goal of the paper and respond to the following: Did the authors accomplish their goal? Is there anything missing or anything you would have liked to have seen them do better?

*Figure 6.2.* Assignment for article critique. (Used with permission, C. Masiello, personal communication, May 24, 2012).

Assessment Rubric
**Organic Geochemistry Writing Assignment in Response to Grice et al. (2005)**
*10 points*

**Name:** _____

|  | Yes | No |
|---|---|---|
| **Part 1: You included all required components of the assignment.** <br> • Vocabulary <br> • Statement of paper's goals <br> • Conclusion of paper <br> • Effective quote choice | | |
| **Part 2: You included all required components of the assignment.** <br> • Geological time period <br> • Marker structure/function <br> • Method <br> • Cholorbiaceae | | |

|  | Strong | Developing | Weak | Items that need attention |
|---|---|---|---|---|
| You reported information clearly and accurately and used it to back up your ideas. | | | | |
| You thoughtfully compared the authors' goals with their conclusions, identified any points where goals were not completely met (uncertainties in the author's methods or logic), and effectively explained your interpretation. | | | | |

*Figure 6.3.* Assessment rubric for article critique. (Used with permission, C. Masiello, personal communication, May 24, 2012).

## The FAQ

Requiring the same type of research as a more traditional academic paper, the FAQ (i.e., frequently asked questions) is a highly reader-driven informational document in a well organized, designed, and dynamic package (Strickland, 2004). Writers must imagine the topic and information from the point of view of the reader to construct questions, synthesize research, and arrange it (i.e., columns, hyperlinks, and sidebars) to meet the user's needs. The FAQ can stand by itself as a technical document or as a shorter piece within the research portfolio that helps support the development of a longer document. Where possible, instructors might ask that the FAQ be published on the Internet, giving students an opportunity to write for an audience beyond their instructor and peers. For example, students developing a policy proposal for a community agency might draft an FAQ on the new policy for hosting on the agency's website. Feedback from real readers may provide invaluable information to students to help them not only revise the FAQ but also rethink the questions, assumptions, and conclusions driving the development of their independent research project. Figure 6.4 offers an example of an FAQ assignment with an emphasis on audience awareness.

## Blogs

Writing online blogs allows students to try on the voice and persona of an authority in their subject and discipline, while developing technological skills that may become part of their postgraduation lives. Individual assignments can be posted to a blog, or students can use a blogging platform for organizing and producing the entire research portfolio. Miller and Shepherd (2004) noted that there are two primary types of blogs—those that filter and annotate content (primarily Internet content) and those given to personal expression, which are more common. The filter-type blog is likely to be more appropriate for the senior seminar, but Miller and Shepherd suggested that the lines between the two are frequently blurred. In fact, "what many bloggers find most compelling about blogs is the ability to combine the immediately real and the genuinely personal" (Whatis.com, 2003, quoted in Miller & Shepherd, Semantic Content and Substance section, para. 4). Moreover, the presence of links in blog posts binds the blogger to others in the virtual discourse community (Hourihan, 2002, cited in Miller & Shepherd, 2004). The immediacy, potentially personal, and interconnected nature of blog writing means students must be prepared to confront the effect of language choices on their readers' experiences in ways that may not be required in other genres. Such awareness may help them understand how and why writers make more formal and standardized choices in style and voice in other settings for other audiences.

*Overview:* In this project, you will write an FAQ on a topic of your choice. This assignment will develop your awareness of how to conduct and present research to meet your readers' needs.

### Part I. Find your topic and questions.

1. List possible choices for the subject of your FAQ.

2. List possible questions for your FAQ by thinking about the controversies in this subject.

3. Choose one item from your list, and do some general research on this topic. Find out ways in which this topic is presented to the general Internet reading population. Imagine the kinds of questions readers have about this topic.

### Part II. Research your topic.

1. On one page, make a preliminary list of the information you want to communicate to readers in your FAQ. On another page, list 5-10 questions you imagine other readers could have.

2. Create an audience profile for your FAQ: How much does your reader already know on this topic? What are they likely to care about that connects to your topic?

### Part III. Design the FAQ.

1. Draft a set of questions and answers for your FAQ, integrating information from your research. Discuss as a class whether or not readers want to see in-text citations in a FAQ or would be satisfied to see a list of sources at the end of the document. Look at examples online and describe the ways authors cite their sources in FAQs.

2. Review your draft with a partner or a small group, discussing organizational possibilities. Look at sample FAQs and describe the structures you find. What questions do writers use at the beginning of the document to establish authority and credibility?

3. Draft your FAQ using your preliminary organizational structure, considering the particular understanding of the topic you would like your reader to develop and the best structure for leading them to that understanding.

4. Exchange these drafts in small groups, and evaluate the effectiveness of the order of the questions.

5. Revise your FAQ to improve its effectiveness, and enhance the document with links to information as well as appealing visuals. Be sure to credit any graphic material that you insert into your document.

6. Evaluate the overall balance of your document. Determine adjustments in spacing, placement of graphics, and length of questions and answers to give the document a clean, easy-to-read, balanced visual impact.

7. Review your almost-final draft with your small group, focusing on clarity of expression in your answers. Read the questions and answers aloud, listening for overly long sentences, as well as unclear phrases.

*Figure 6.4.* FAQ assignment overview.

## Conclusion

Students face problems when they encounter the independent research project in the senior seminar. First, they must identify and effectively narrow a question for further exploration. Students also need tools to help them evaluate responses to similar questions that might have bearing on their project. Finally, they may have limited practice in making decisions about which technical modalities and written genres will be most effective for reaching a particular audience and achieving a specific purpose. The I-Search process and the research portfolio are two strategies that can help students navigate these challenges as they conceptualize and engage in the research process. The chapter that follows describes ways to facilitate writing up the research project and other types of formal academic papers in the senior capstone.

# Chapter 7

## A Range of Persuasive Purposes in Academic Discourse

In a 2012 *New York Times* article, Judith Martin (better known as Miss Manners) suggested the dinner party is endangered not because people no longer cook for others but because conversations are in trouble: "People have been brought up to express themselves rather than to exchange ideas" (Trebay, 2012). Arguably, preparing students to exchange ideas is one of the purposes of higher education, but the academic environment may work against this goal at times. As Doerr-Stevens, Beach, and Boeser (2011) noted, "traditional persuasive writing ... typically involves formulating arguments and supporting evidence to convince" an audience (p. 33). That audience is most frequently the instructor, as she or he likely will be the only person to read and respond to a student's argument. Further, this focus on convincing an audience is decidedly a one-way street, with little opportunity for any voices beyond the students' to shape the conclusions drawn. Traditional approaches to teaching argument, coupled with examples from the media and politics, also may reinforce the notion that to be persuasive is to be combative; agonistic; or aggressive in tone, voice, and strategy (Rex, Thomas, & Engel, 2010).

Yet, Williams and McGee (2000) concluded such approaches to argument might actually inhibit critical thinking. Because a student could be focused on winning rather than coming up with the best possible solution to an ill-structured problem, he or she may overlook or undervalue evidence or perspectives that do not conform with his or her position (cf., Veerman, Andriessen, & Kanselaar, 2002). Drawing on feminist values of consensus building and shared power in problem solving (Lamb, 1991), collaborative approaches to argument consider the perspectives of a range of possible audiences and weigh "the merits of competing positions, refuting arguments as false or not supported, and moving toward some recommended synthesis or solution" (Doerr-Steven et al., 2011, p. 33). As such, they help foster "reflection and deep thinking" and promote understanding of "knowledge as a process of permanent negotiation" (Veerman et al., 2002, p. 155). Further, argumentation is an important function of a democratic society, allowing citizens to assert their opinions in relationship to people with whom they live and work. In fact, the skills and disposition gained through exposure to collaborative or cooperative argument lay the groundwork for successful performance in the diverse environments of the workplace and society.

Thus far, this discussion of argument has assumed that persuasive writing involves explicit appeals to adopt certain positions, implement policies, or take specific actions. While students need practice in developing this type of persuasive piece, they also need to understand the more subtle forms of persuasion that exist within academic writing. Persuasive or argumentative elements can be found in many kinds of writing, including discourse that is primarily informative, but also designed to move an audience to a new understanding of a topic. For example, the student developing a proposal for a senior project must present a compelling rationale for looking at a particular issue at this specific moment. Moreover, he or she needs to suggest why certain methodologies are most appropriate for exploring the questions at hand. Once the research project is underway, students must convince readers that their interpretations of the data and conclusions drawn are both valid and valuable.

Meltzer (2009) found in his national study of more than 2,000 writing assignments from college courses, including senior seminars, that writing to inform (also known as *transactional writing*) is the dominant function required by faculty in a variety of disciplines. Fulwiler and Jones (1982) identified book reviews, lab reports, proposals, and dissertations as forms of transactional writing in educational settings. In the workplace, transactional writing includes letters, memos, abstracts, summaries, proposals, reports, and other planning documents. Asking students, therefore, to practice transactional writing along a spectrum of persuasiveness will help prepare them for workplace writing and should contribute to their abilities to advance in their careers.

This chapter examines the range of skills students need to make successful arguments in academic conversations—skills that transfer to workplace and civic settings following graduation. More specifically, classroom-based activities and writing assignments that will support the development of these skills are described.

## Skills Supporting Persuasive Writing

This section examines two different but related approaches to argument in academic settings. The first, based in the classical rhetorical tradition, views argument as the attempt to persuade an audience to adopt a particular position or to take some type of action. The second views academic argument not so much as an effort to win an audience over to a particular position as to negotiate new understandings and meanings. Here, authors persuade readers of the validity and usefulness of their ideas by using a standard set of moves to engage a range of ideas in developing and supporting their positions.

### *Traditional Rhetorical Approaches*

According to Aristotle (trans. 1991), rhetoric "allows one to debate both sides of an issue … to help the speaker understand the real state of the case and be able to refute an opponent" (p. 14). For Aristotle, the real value in this understanding was not in its capacity to persuade but in the ability to "see the available means of persuasion in each case" (p. 35). These means of persuasion might be largely thought of as two types—those that exist outside the writer or speaker (i.e., *inartistic proofs*) and those that the writer or speaker invents (i.e., *artistic proofs*). The former consists of facts that exist beforehand, such as findings from previous studies, raw empirical data, images, video or audio clips, and quotes. While this material is a necessary condition for successful academic writing, it is hardly sufficient. Decisions about how to present and organize the material and the conclusions drawn from it determine the success of a piece of writing. In Aristotle's rhetoric, such decisions are guided by the three artistic proofs: *ethos* (appeals to character), *logos* (appeals to reason), and *pathos* (appeals to emotion).

In academic writing, focusing on the character of the writer (i.e., presenting oneself as a knowledgeable member of a disciplinary community) and the development of logical arguments are typically privileged over emotional appeals. Faculty may have greater comfort with explaining and modeling logical appeals, but they must also help students understand how stylistic choices—from sentence structure to spelling—shape readers' perceptions of their credibility. As writers choose how they express, explain, and justify their beliefs or claims, they manifest their values. In turn, these language choices affect the relationship between the writer and his or her readers and, ultimately, the overall success of the document in achieving its purpose. Ethos, or the character of the speaker or writer, therefore, is a keystone for the choices writers make: How do we want to sound to our reader when we explain our beliefs? Who do we want our reader to think we are? and What kind of person are we representing to our reader through our choices?

Because of the powerful connections among personal identity, values, and writing, students may dismiss an instructor's evaluation of a text with a comment such as, "He just does not like my style." A rhetorical approach to understanding argument, with its emphasis on strategies for making effective choices to stake and explain a claim, will help students analyze their style and voice more objectively by asking questions such as, What did I do to detract from my credibility through choices I made in informal or formal language? and How did I incorporate references from respected authorities in order to borrow their authority for my own argument?

As instructors introduce different genres in the discipline, they will want to help students consider the relative value of each of these appeals—character, logic, emotions—within a specific genre. For instance, reports of empirical research in the hard sciences and the social sciences would emphasize logical appeals, although students might incorporate character appeals through careful reviews of the literature. An upper-level public relations writing course at the University of South Carolina engaged in writing news releases, media alerts, fact sheets, communications audits, and public service announcements (PSAs) to support a Curing Kids Cancer event (Hall, 2012). While many of these genres are not inherently persuasive, the instructor could engage the class in a discussion of how emphasizing emotional appeals in the PSAs might garner more support for the charity event than a strict reliance on logical appeals would.

Asking students to perform a rhetorical analysis of a published article or model text provides them with insight into how appeals to character, logic, and emotions typically are handled within specific disciplinary communities and genres. Figure 7.1 offers a set of questions to help guide a rhetorical analysis. Instructors can customize the questions to foreground the types of appeals that are most customary or most valued for in a particular discipline. Such questions might be used to guide small-group discussions of texts or to shape brief, informal writing assignments.

As noted above, artistic proofs arise from within or are invented by the writer. In addition to reading widely in the literature, designing proposals for study, and collecting and analyzing data, students will need to determine which appeals, and combination of appeals, are most effective in communicating their ideas to an audience. As such, having students spend some time exploring possibilities

**Assignment:** Rhetorical analysis of published article or text

*Ethos:*
- What personal information, stories, or observations does the writer use to help build his or her ethos?
- Describe the general ethos of the writer. Explain how this character or persona is appropriate for the purpose of the essay.
- How is this characterization of himself or herself relevant to his or her main claim?
- Where does the writer undermine his or her own ethos?

*Logos:*
- Where does the writer include appeals to logic that are especially convincing?
- Describe the different kinds of logical appeals the writer uses (e.g., personal experiences, interviews, scientific data, historical background). On which of these appeals does the writer rely most? Why do you think the writer chose this appeal as the dominant form?
- How does the writer use logical appeals to build credibility for his or her argument?
- Where do you find logical appeals that are out-of-date or from unreliable sources?
- How does reliance on less credible sources affect his or her main claim?

*Pathos:*
- Where does the writer appeal to our emotions to persuade us of his or her idea?
- What is the effect of engaging our emotions in this way?
- What is your evaluation of being manipulated emotionally by the writer?
- Why has the writer chosen not to use emotional appeals?

*Connecting Ethos, Logos, and Pathos to Overall Effectiveness:*
- How does the writer's ethos influence the way you evaluate the logos in his or her argument?
- How does the writer's use of pathos color your view of his or her ethos?
- What specific examples of ethos, logos, and pathos positively affect your evaluation of the writer's main claim? Which ones affect it negatively?
- What choices did the writer make that you would consider replicating in your own writing? How would you incorporate these choices in your work?

*Figure 7.1.* Sample questions for a rhetorical analysis.

before they begin writing can be especially helpful. The questions in Figure 7.2 offer a rhetorical invention strategy that might be used throughout the drafting process to help students assess the effectiveness of their writing. As with the questions for rhetorical analysis, instructors may wish to customize them to more clearly communicate disciplinary conventions and expectations.

---

**Assignment:** Use the invention questions below to help plan and/or evaluate your draft.

***Ethos:***
- What personal information, stories, or observations can I use to help build my ethos?
- How is this characterization of myself relevant to my main claim?
- What do I need to revise stylistically to improve my ethos? What choices have I made in informal language (e.g., slang) that result in vague explanations of my ideas? How have I incorporated the language of my discipline in order to strengthen my ethos?

***Logos:***
- What information do I need to research in order to appeal to logos in my argument?
- Where should I use logos to build credibility for my argument?
- What appeals to logos might my reader judge to be out-of-date, untrustworthy, or from an unreliable source?

***Pathos:***
- Where would it be appropriate to appeal to emotions in my argument?
- What will be the effect on the reader of my use of pathos? Why might my reader find this use of pathos objectionable?
- What kinds of stories and observations could I use as appeals to pathos?

---

*Figure 7.2.* Rhetorical invention strategy.

Classical rhetorical models help outline argumentation patterns, especially within disciplines for which prescribed forms do not exist (e.g., a literary analysis vs. a report of a social science research study). Students can use organizational guidelines when they begin drafting, helping them plan the presentation and arrangement of their supporting assumptions, information, explanations, and research. The same guidelines also will direct students to read their drafts (or their classmates' drafts) for the required components.

A sample guide is presented in Figure 7.3, but instructors will want to identify and reproduce guides that reflect common disciplinary genres so that students are well supported in communicating their senior capstone projects (see Figure 7.4, p. 100, for examples). Whatever guide instructors provide, it should include notes about the purpose of each section, allowing students to make intentional choices as they draft rather than merely complete a template. Further, students need to understand the guide is only a suggested structure and sections can be moved and reshaped to suit individual purposes. For example, in Figure 7.3, the refutation of alternate perspectives comes after the confirmation

**Argumentative Document: Organizational Guidelines**

***Introduction:*** Orient your reader to your document. Introduce the subject and your authority around it. Create interest in your subject and your perspective.
* Introduce the subject you are discussing.
* Establish your own authority and credibility by briefly explaining your relationship to the subject or why you care about this issue.
* Create interest in your issue and point of view by connecting to your reader's experiences, perspectives, and opinions.

***Partition:*** Help the reader predict the organization of your material, the rationale of your argument, and the general scope of your supporting material.
* Explain the purpose and scope of your document.
* State your claim (main idea, thesis, or primary assertion).
* Describe what you intend to do in this document.
* Identify the rationale or logic in your position on the subject.

***Narration:*** Describe the history of this issue so that your reader understands the broader social, cultural, economic, practical, or personal context. Choose from the list below, as appropriate, for the purpose of your argument, report, or proposal.
* Provide necessary historical background information about how this issue developed.
* Incorporate relevant research pertaining to the history of your topic.
* Identify any current laws or practices that contribute to understanding this issue.
* Explain the problems with the status quo of this issue.
* Explain how your solution addresses problems in the status quo.
* Define your criteria for evaluating the current situation as problematic or in need of some kind of change.

***Confirmation:*** Explain, in depth, your reasons supporting your claim or main idea (thesis).
* Explain each of your reasons one at a time for your point of view.
* Use at least one full paragraph for each main reason behind your argument.
* Create headings to help the reader remember the connection between your main idea (claim or thesis) and the evidence you are discussing that supports it.

***Respectful Refutation:*** Acknowledge other perspectives on this issue to establish a diverse range of points of view and indicate that you have considered the topic from angles other than the one you are promoting.
* Discuss each alternate perspective in a separate paragraph.
* Explain the merit of each alternate perspective.
* Explain, by comparing and contrasting, how your point of view addresses the importance of the issue more fully than the alternative perspectives.
* If possible, suggest connections among your perspective and the alternate ones. Suggest how multiple visions of the issue can be compatible.

***Conclusion:*** Inspire your reader to connect to your point of view and believe your argument.
* Summarize your key points, highlighting the most important details of your argument and your supporting materials.
* Suggest how your point of view impacts the future of this issue and its effect on individuals, society, history, culture, or our understanding of the world.
* Return to key words, phrases, images, or ideas from your introduction, helping the reader remember the general importance of your point of view and providing incentive for your reader to take action as you are proposing.

*Figure 7.3.* Rhetorical model for argument.

or presentation of the student's main argument. However, acknowledging other perspectives might just as easily become part of the narration, or description of the history of the issue. Rather than comparing their solution to previous ones (i.e., the order suggested by Figure 7.3), raising other perspectives early in the argument allows students to use what they consider to be inadequate or partial solutions as a motivating factor for their current investigation.

### Standard Academic Moves

While the strategies Aristotle and later rhetoricians described were meant to support the development of ideas across a wide range of disciplines, communities of practice have created specific forms for communicating knowledge among their members. In addition to overarching organizational schemes, these forms also encompass a standard set of moves, or tacit plans or approaches to writing and speaking. A discussion of all the genres that have evolved (and that will continue to evolve with the advent of new technologies) is beyond the scope of this book, but this section highlights a handful of standard strategies for communication within academic communities. The authors are indebted to Graff and Birkenstein (2010) who have created an excellent primer on basic moves students need to master to make successful arguments in academic and civic spheres. These moves include

- *Using what others say as a motivation for writing.* As Graff and Birkenstein noted, "the best academic writing … is deeply engaged in some way with other people's views" (p. 3). Students must be able to situate their argument by effectively paraphrasing, summarizing, quoting, or debating the ideas to which they are responding.

- *Clearly stating a position as a response to what others say.* Graff and Birkenstein suggested three basic responses exist within academic writing: (a) disagreement, (b) agreement, and (c) simultaneous disagreement and agreement. For students, the challenge is moving beyond these basic responses (i.e., I agree with X, or I disagree with Y) to craft a more subtle argument. Thus, simple disagreement must be supplemented with an explanation as to why the position responded to is inadequate, based on faulty assumptions, supportive of contrary positions, and so on. Positions of agreement must bring new information or perspective to bear rather than merely echo what earlier authors have said.

- *Adequately distinguishing the voices in the conversation.* Concerns about academic integrity aside, students may struggle to differentiate their own ideas and positions from the larger conversations to which they are responding. Such struggles may be exacerbated by the mistaken idea that it is never appropriate to use the first person in academic writing. Instructors can model disciplinary-appropriate ways for using first person and incorporating what Graff and Birkenstein called voice markers (i.e., overt and subtle cues as to who is speaking in a text).

- *Anticipating and responding to objections.* Students who write successful academic arguments imagine "what others might say against [their] argument as it unfolds" (p. 79) and use that opposition to refine their thinking. To craft academic arguments effectively, they will need practice in presenting objective summaries of likely opposing arguments and making concessions without undermining their own position.

- *Establishing the significance of the argument.* Graff and Birkenstein argued that the two questions every writer must answer are Who cares? and So what? The former speaks to the individuals or groups who are likely to have a stake in the argument. For the student in the senior capstone, these readers may be his or her disciplinary community or a small portion of that community engaged in a specific type of inquiry. If the capstone involves service-learning or practica experience, the audience for the argument may be a particular client or individuals served by a local agency. The latter question asks students to "link [their] argument to some larger matter that readers already deem important" (p. 97). In particular, students must suggest why their exploration of an issue matters and why it is important to examine it currently.

As with the Aristotelian proofs described earlier, these moves can be useful to help students generate material for their drafts. To that end, Graff and Birkenstein (2010) offer templates, allowing students simply to fill in the blanks to organize their thinking and writing on a topic. Figure 7.4 highlights selected templates students might adopt to accomplish specific goals in a piece of writing.

Graff and Birkenstein's templates provide guidance on how to organize the text on a micro level, but students may still need guidance on strategies for shaping a piece of writing on a larger scale. Figure 7.5 offers two templates for academic genres students might encounter in the senior capstone—a report of empirical research and an analytic essay in the social sciences.

| Standard Move | Possible Templates |
|---|---|
| Disagreeing with reasons | • X's claim that _____ rests upon the questionable assumption that _____.<br><br>• By focusing on _____, X overlooks the deeper problem of _____. |
| Agreeing with a difference | • X's theory of _____ is extremely useful because it provides insight on the difficult problem of _____.<br><br>• If group X is right that _____, as I think they are, then we need to reassess the popular assumption that _____. |
| Agreeing and disagreeing simultaneously | • Although I disagree with much that X says, I fully endorse his final conclusion that _____.<br><br>• Though I concede that _____, I still insist that _____. |
| Embedding voice markers | • I wholeheartedly endorse what X calls _____.<br><br>• These conclusions, which X discusses in _____, add weight to the argument that _____. |
| Indicating who cares | • These findings challenge the work of earlier researchers, who tended to assume that _____.<br><br>• Recent studies like these shed new light on _____, which previous studies had not addressed. |
| Establishing why claims matter | • Although X may seem trivial, it is, in fact, crucial in terms of today's concern over _____.<br><br>• This discovery will have significant applications in _____ as well as in _____. |

*Figure 7.4.* Templates for basic moves in academic discourse. Adapted from *They Say/I Say: The Moves that Matter in Academic Writing*, by G. Graff and C. Birkenstein, 2010, pp. 225-231. Copyright 2010 by W. W. Norton and Company, Inc.

**Writing Reports of Empirical Research**

*Abstract*
- Offers brief overview of study and key findings

*Introduction and Literature Review*
- Defines the problem under study and describes its significance
- Places the current study in context by describing dominant theories and data supporting them to which research responds
- Identifies gaps in the literature to which current study responds

*Materials and Methods*
- Describes methods used to collect data
- Identifies rationale for selecting specific data collection methods

*Results*
- Summarizes data, providing information related to sample size, units of measure, degree of variability, and other factors to help situate findings
- Includes tables, graphs, and figures to synthesize large data sets

*Discussion*
- Explains what data mean within reasonable probability
- Puts findings in context, comparing them to those of similar research studies
- Suggests whether findings from current study confirm, challenge, or refine prevailing theories or findings from similar studies
- Suggests new questions findings raise
- Identifies limitations of current study and suggests strategies for resolving them in future studies
- Suggests significance of findings

**Writing Essays in the Social Sciences**

*Introduction and Thesis*
- Identifies and describes topic, suggests who has a stake in it and why reader should care about it
- Takes a specific stand on the topic, situating that stand in the ongoing conversation of the literature and suggesting what new or significant ideas this argument will add to the conversation
- Offers outline of the argument to follow

*Literature Review*
- Offers overview of scholarly work on a topic
- Identifies prominent themes in the scholarly work
- Outlines competing interpretations or theories

*Analysis*
- Presents evidence and arguments in support of the thesis
- Uses data (e.g., surveys, interviews, first-person accounts) to suport thesis
- Acknowledges and responds to possible objections

*Conclusion*
- Describes implications and makes recommendations for action, policy changes, and/or future research
- Suggests what problems and questions remain
- Suggests significance of findings

*Figure 7.5.* Templates for writing in the sciences and social sciences.

## Using Peer-Group Conversation to Shape Academic Discourse

One way to improve instruction in argumentative writing is to take advantage of students' oral communication skills through more peer-talk time. Rehearsing new ideas in small groups or pairs strengthens students' arguments by building confidence, expanding understanding of different perspectives, and refining points. Informal conversations give students the chance to describe supporting data for their claims and try out provisional interpretations. Such opportunities may be particularly important for students whose conclusions may lead to an unpopular opinion on a controversial topic. Students also may face internal conflict when they commit to an idea, worrying that they may be wrong (Lynch, George, & Cooper, 1997). Talking about their ideas with peers can lead to discoveries that others share the same apprehension.

Small-group workshops that direct students to hear alternative perspectives will help writers develop written arguments that are more complete, just, and reasonable. When students discover ways to develop arguments through a multiplicity of perspectives gained during peer-group discussion, their written arguments will be more democratic, evolving from a mutual construction of knowledge. In addition, they hear the kinds of alternate views that may need to be integrated into their own arguments, especially if alternatives suggest important differences that demand a rebuttal. Faculty conferences with students also can be a forum for helping students consider divergent viewpoints. For example, Chris Schneider notes that the mechanical engineering professor who led his senior seminar was "really good at asking tough questions about data or reasons to back up our statements" (personal communication, September 3, 2012). As a result, he developed the habit of anticipating questions from his audience (as listeners or readers), which has stayed with him at work today, leading him to develop an additional slide for PowerPoint presentations that specifically lists questions and answers.

Finally, small-group conversation can be integral to developing disciplinary identity, a frequent goal of senior capstones as noted in chapter 1. Rafoth (1988) explained that *argument fields*, contexts based on shared standards and community norms for communication, help us understand how the discourse takes place, how it developed, and how we can evaluate it. Being in a community that shares parameters for argument provides students an opportunity to explore and practice the entire context of the argument within a discipline. In other words, small-group conversations help students engage in the social enterprise by reading, writing, and talking in disciplinary-specific ways.

A doctoral candidate in mathematics at the University of California at Berkeley described his introduction to the argument field of mathematics as including weekly meetings with advisors on his undergraduate thesis, regular opportunities to talk with his peers about the process of writing his thesis, and a final lecture when his thesis was completed (A. Kruckman, personal communication, September 4, 2012). He stated,

> The field of math is really all about communication: a proof, the primary component of pure math, is a communication of clear and indisputable reasons why a certain fact is true. ... The bottom line is it is incredibly important for a mathematician to be able to communicate his or her ideas to the community. Math has its own very specialized language and set of presentation conventions, so part of learning to communicate is learning to communicate *in a mathematical way*—so that other mathematicians can decipher it, understand it, and take it seriously. (A. Kruckman, personal communication, September 4, 2012)

Instructors can facilitate this disciplinary talk through discussion guides that ask students to think about and incorporate the language of the argument field into their informal conversations with peers and group work. For example, students might be directed to consider questions such as, How would an expert discuss this controversy? What key terms would we expect an expert to use? and What would an expert need to explain to a general audience? Faculty should expect that students will blend formal disciplinary terms with informal conversation, both in style and content. This blending allows students to absorb elements of their disciplinary identity into their whole self-concepts.

## Proposal Writing: Academic Argument in Action

Pegram (2006) noted that a well-researched and documented proposal is a "mode for students to properly use research as a tool for solving real-life problems with creative-thinking skills" (p. 21). Because proposals can take many forms and address a variety of topics, they are appropriate as major writing assignments in a wide range of senior capstones. Proposal writing might include the justification and design of an empirical research study, a grant application, graduate school fellowship applications, or a business plan, among other academic and technical documents. This genre also demands a balance of informative and persuasive discourse, with an overarching transactional purpose. For example, students in an anthropology capstone at IUP researched and identified a program in an area of interest, then drafted a proposal (which they were not required to send) to a faculty member in that field, arguing they would make worthy contributions to the program because of their past experiences and interests (L. Kruckman, personal communication, April 25, 2011). In addition, the project helped demystify the graduate school application process and encouraged students to think of themselves as candidates for a graduate program in anthropology. Students could also use this process to write a cover letter for a desired professional position. The assignment allowed them to work with the genre in a low-risk context in which they could easily ask for and receive feedback on their application materials before having to send them out for formal review.

Kalivas (2008) described a lab proposal project in a chemistry course at Idaho State University. Working in teams, students "design all aspects of a discovery-lab experiment to teach a chemical concept as if they were the instructor" (p. 1412), including a literature review and teaching guide. Draft proposals were critiqued by other teams and were then revised before being presented orally to the class. Class members voted on the lab proposal that best met the assignment criteria, and students conducted this lab during the last week of class. The project encompassed "science process skills," which included "searching, reading, and evaluating literature; articulating a research question; designing an experiment; formulating scientific explanations using experimental evidence; and effectively communicating the results of a scientific investigation" (Kalivas, p. 1410). As Kalivas noted, graduate admissions committees and employers value these skills, but new graduates often lack them.

Reave (2002) used the internal proposal—a genre also identified in business writing as a justification report, completed in memo form—to help students become active contributors as employees. Because organizations expect employees to be ready to write, Reave argued that students need to gain experience researching, creating, and finalizing proposals, which demands a high level of critical thinking. The proposal might be the end product of a service-learning placement, internship, or practicum experience, and proposals developed in consultation with local organizations or businesses can lead to successful real-world connections.

While a proposal might constitute a culminating project for the senior seminar in itself, it might also serve as a launching point for a capstone experience—especially if the capstone is a two-semester course. Hawke (1983) reported on a two-course biology sequence at Willamette University in which juniors developed an annotated bibliography and prospectus for a research study to complete in the senior seminar. The proposal might also figure as a component in a larger portfolio of work students complete in a capstone course. In an electrical engineering seminar described by Ostheimer and White (2005), students were required to "write a proposal to perform a project, undertake research, develop a program, solicit funding, or some combination of the above" (p. 64). The proposal was incorporated into the course portfolio, which also included a letter or memorandum selling the idea to an audience and "a professionally written design report" (p. 64).

Figure 7.6 offers guidelines for writing a proposal for a major project, asking students to synthesize research and argue for a specific opinion on a topic. Proposals frequently are treated as informal writing assignments—both by students and instructors. Yet, if a goal of the senior capstone is to help students master a genre they may encounter again in graduate school or in the workforce, then they should be encouraged to plan and revise these documents with the same level of care as with the final project. Informal writing assignments, based on the following questions, can offer students a way to explore and plan their proposals and research:

- Why does your topic matter to you, and why is it important? What personal experiences have you had with this topic that make you want to know more about it?

- How do you intend to explore the topic? How will you interest your reader in your topic and opinion? How will you consider your reader's beliefs about your topic? What kind of appeals will help your reader understand your perspective?

- What kinds of research do you plan to do? What surveys or databases might you consider? Who could you interview by e-mail or in person on campus?

- Are there sources in your research portfolio that will be useful in your project?

- What research topics do you need to investigate more fully?

- Are there any financial costs you expect to incur through your research (e.g., photocopying, printing, communication costs)?

- What will your timeline look like, including researching, conferencing, drafting, interviewing, revising, editing a final draft, and preparing a presentation?

- What difficulties might make your work more challenging, and how would you face these challenges?

### Guidelines for the Proposal for the Major Project

*Cover Page:* Name, title, course name, and date.

#### Part I: Background Materials

1. **Executive summary.** Write two or three paragraphs summarizing the document's purpose, supporting evidence, and conclusions. Imagine that you are writing for a busy administrator who needs to skim the document quickly and wants the key points up front.

2. **Introduction.** Begin the body of the document with an introduction establishing the nature of the problem being investigated.
   a) Explain the main idea using a professional voice and style; avoid technical language that would be unfamiliar to a reader not in the discipline.
   b) Conclude by emphasizing the benefits of the findings (e.g., how the proposed solution offers a new way of understanding the problem).

3. **Rationale.** Explain how the solution will solve important problems raised by people in the larger disciplinary community.
   a) Include your own observations and experiences to build bridges with your reader.
   b) Select one effective and short narrative to function as an example of how you have experienced this problem.
   c) Identify the most crucial research supporting the proposed solutions. Ensure this research is current, credible, and cited appropriately.

#### Part II: In-Depth Consideration of the Project

1. **Synthesis of Research.** Provide a review of relevant research.
   a) The review of research should fit analytically with the rest of the document. Use headings to build connections between the key points about the research and your main ideas.
   b) Organize the discussion of research relevant to the solution according to the conventions of the discipline, which may be thematic or chronological, so that the reader develops an analytical perspective on the history of this problem, past solutions, and the proposed solution.
   c) Build an argument for the project by explaining how it is ethical, just, reasonable, affordable (if applicable), and timely. Use logical appeals to demonstrate the ethics of the solution. Remember that presenting yourself as a reasonable thinker boosts your credibility and trustworthiness, which aids the overall argumentation.

#### Part III. Execution of the Project

1. **Resources.** Identify any resources needed to proceed with the investigation (e.g., money to support field or lab research, interviews with experts, travel costs). Describe any contributions received to support the research.

2. **Timeline.** Develop a timeline for completing the project, ensuring that deadlines are reasonable.

3. **Difficulties.** Identify possible difficulties you foresee in the timeline and indicate strategies for problem solving.

---

**Part IV. Conclusion**
Remind the reader of the value of the project, but enhance this perspective by suggesting how this project is important for the greater good. Consider strategies such as illustrating how the solution improves life for those affected by the problem.

**Part V. Appendices**
Insert documents in this section as they are completed (e.g., interview reports, surveys, references or works cited list, charts or graphs). Make sure that all documents are linked to materials in the major proposal.

---

*Figure 7.6.* Outline for proposal for senior capstone project.

Because proposals are highly structured, students approach them with problems in organization and arrangement partly solved, freeing them to focus on developing their argument and demonstrating authority on a topic. At the same time, they are more than simple, fill-in-the-blank documents. Instead, students must engage in sophisticated rhetorical problem solving with respect to audience, purpose, and style. As such, proposals are excellent sources for facilitating intellectual growth while helping students improve their disciplinary communication skills.

## Conclusion

The major project in the senior capstone can encompass a variety of genres (e.g., a report of an empirical research study, an analytic essay, a policy proposal, a technical report). Whatever form the project takes, students likely will be expected to persuade readers in some way—if not to take a specific action, then at least to consider and value the position they present. To be successful, students must master a range of argumentative moves that are standard in academic writing. Many of these same moves translate to the professional and civic roles in which students may find themselves after graduation. Helping students master strategies for developing and presenting well-reasoned arguments serves the academic purposes of senior capstones while also supporting students' personal and intellectual development.

# Chapter 8

## Oral Presentations: Unifying Spoken and Written Communication

On many campuses, oral presentations accompany the completion of major projects in the senior capstone. From a 1999 survey, Henscheid (2000) reported that 75.1% of capstone courses required an oral presentation. A more recent study conducted by the National Resource Center for The First-Year Experience and Students in Transition (Padgett & Kilgo, 2012) found that 28% of institutions offering senior seminars listed improving oral communication skills as an important course objective and almost half (47.4%) required a final presentation as an end product of the capstone experience. Further, as mentioned in chapter 1, employers ranked strong oral communication skills among the most desirable characteristics for new employees while at the same time noting new hires are not well prepared in this area. Yet, as with writing, faculty may be reluctant to incorporate opportunities to develop oral communication skills in the senior capstone. Shaw (1999) listed several reasons for this resistance: (a) presentation skills are not a primary focus of the course; (b) presentations are difficult to schedule; and (c) they take time away from instruction on important topics. Yet, Shaw countered that "letting students speak on academic topics not only raises their presentation consciousness and skills but also reinforces their mastery of material" (p. 154). This chapter offers guidance on ways to incorporate student talk that supports both the development of important academic and professional skills and the mastery of course content.

In keeping with the larger theme of the book, the chapter also examines the links between written and oral communication, describing the ways that writing can support the development of strong presentations and how they might facilitate more effective writing. Although not all presentations may require written components, it can be assumed they all require a substantial level of planning, drafting, and revising—just as formal written assignments do. The chapter describes the range of skills encompassed in oral communication and strategies for helping students develop those skills.

## Oral Communication Skills

This volume has emphasized the value of peer talk for improving students' writing and critical thinking. Through collaborative development sessions and peer review workshops, students are exposed to different perspectives that help them clarify their own positions. Small-group discussions—especially when resulting in some type of product—give students practice in valuable interpersonal skills, such as listening, negotiation, and cooperation. Similarly, oral presentations can support the development of the kinds of interpersonal skills valued by employers. Students learn how to read an audience's bodily and facial expressions to make adjustments in pacing or tone, as well as how to respond to challenging questions. More generally, they gain practice in communicating information— some of it highly technical—to faculty, peers, and others. Students typically also gain practice in standard patterns of professional communication, such as poster sessions or podium talks in academic disciplines, client presentations in business or technical fields, or teaching demonstrations in education fields.

Oral presentations on major projects will, like written products, vary in their persuasive effect. In some courses, it may be more appropriate for students to report on their research findings rather than establish an argument about the ways in which their research, for example, supports a controversial position. Presentations that emphasize information rather than an opinion or argument still challenge students' critical-thinking abilities as they seek to sort, organize, and develop material purposefully. In fact, the act of preparing information for presentation to a specific audience challenges students to consider major rhetorical questions that engage critical thinking, such as What background information does my audience need to know to understand the new material I wish to share? What is the best way to arrange my information for this audience so that they can follow the development of my ideas? What information will be difficult for my audience to process? and How can I shape the presentation to ensure better understanding? Bazerman (2009) explained that "learned material and new stages of development can influence and restructure what one has previously learned in different ways and in different domains" (p. 285). As students work through these questions, they will move to a new cognitive stage of thinking about the material. The social interaction embedded in preparing a presentation for a specific audience changes the way the writer-speaker engages with and perceives the material and also, as Bazerman noted (2009), moves it from the interpersonal to the intrapersonal plane.

## Incorporating Oral Presentations

A number of opportunities exist for incorporating student presentations into the senior capstone. Two of the most common—the panel or podium presentation and the poster presentation—mirror activities in academic disciplines. In many cases, these presentations accompany the completion of the capstone project and may be delivered as a complement to or in lieu of a formal written report. For example, a biology instructor at Louisiana State University (LSU) had students work in pairs to conduct experiments and then form panels of teams to conduct related experiments and present their findings using PowerPoint (Sullivan, 2009). Fava (2009) reported that LSU also organizes a forum at which science students can present the results of independent research projects on a scientific poster, a larger-format document designed to "quickly and effectively communicate . . . research at a scientific meeting" (Fava & Mangiavellano, n.d.). Whether students are presenting their projects as part of a panel or in poster sessions, departments and colleges or universities often sponsor special events to showcase their work. A number of respondents to the 2011 National Survey of Senior Capstone Experiences described research conferences held in conjunction with senior seminars. Conferences offer opportunities for students to get feedback on their work from their peers, faculty, administrators, or, in some cases, external evaluators. The United States Merchant Marine Academy, Wentworth Institute of Technology, and the University of North Carolina at Charlotte invite high-level industry and/or government personnel to judge and provide feedback on presentations (National Resource Center for The First-Year Experience & Students in Transition, 2011). At Westminster College, classes are cancelled for the Undergraduate Scholars Forum, and students are required to attend as presenters and/or audience members (National Resource Center for The First-Year Experience & Students in Transition, 2011).

Often, student presentations are designed to develop specific job-related communication skills. For example, with the majority of students in a history of mathematics senior seminar at Hood College entering the workforce immediately following graduation (with many becoming teachers), a course objective was to help students "gain confidence in planning a class; giving an oral presentation; [and] making overhead transparencies and handouts"

(Mayfield, 2001, p. 249). Students worked in teams to present the week's topic, dividing the tasks of providing background, proving a famous theorem from the era under study, and either talking about a development in non-Western mathematics during that period or engaging the class in a hands-on activity. All students in the seminar completed a major project accompanied by a presentation, and many math education majors opted to develop a lesson plan (Mayfield, 2001). Similarly, Kalivas (2008) described a service-learning project in an upper-level chemistry course in which teams of students "articulate a research question" and develop a lesson "to effectively communicate scientific explanations" for a K-6 classroom (p. 1413). In addition to presenting the lesson, students created a written report and a poster to leave in the classroom.

In senior capstones focused on synthesizing concepts in the discipline, student presentations might be the primary mode of instruction. The senior seminar in biology at Kean University (Field, 2005) used a case study approach in lieu of more traditional oral presentations and written products. In developing the presentation, students

- "write an original case, using factual information from the primary literature, which includes thought-provoking discussion questions";
- provide guidelines for presenting the case in the classroom setting;
- "deliver an oral presentation in which they familiarize the audience with relevant background information";
- have other students work in small groups to respond to the case study questions; and
- facilitate "an all-class discussion of the case study questions" (Field, 2005, p. 56).

Summarizing the research on using a case approach to instruction, Chan (2011) stated this technique increases student learning and satisfaction, improves critical thinking, and promotes scientific oral communication.

Informational reports also broaden and deepen the scope of a course and help students internalize their learning as they prepare to teach their classmates. In a senior synthesis course on Appalachian culture at IUP, students selected a range of topics for their research and presentations that, by their nature, represented the diversity of experiences found in the region, which helped develop a major purpose of the course—to change attitudes about Appalachian culture, challenge stereotypes, and develop an appreciation for its current richness (J. Cahalan, personal communication, January 21, 2013).

Students also can be given responsibility for preparing and leading class discussions on assigned readings. Shaw (1999) offered two possibilities for organizing such presentations: (a) the *concept anatomy* and (b) *research briefing*. In the concept anatomy, students "define the concept, trace its history, identify its key features, explain it with examples, and apply it to different situations" (Shaw, p. 155). If the assigned reading is a research study, students could prepare a briefing that describes the "rationale, methods, and findings, and evaluate[s] its impact on the issue for which it was referenced" (Shaw, p. 155). Instructors might foreground the goals for synthesizing knowledge by asking students to write memos or journal entries, identifying key ideas from presentations that were interesting, important, or provocative. These informal writing assignments also can be assessment tools for the capstone, providing evidence of relevant concepts and how students integrated this new knowledge. Figure 8.1 offers an example of a culminating reflection memo. To complete the assignment, the students should be encouraged to make notes on presentations throughout the semester or to do brief reflections immediately following them. In this assignment, students write one memo, describing new knowledge they developed as a result of their classmates' investigations. Students select the presentations and the key points they wish to consider based on of the ways the presentations changed their perspective.

---

Select several presentations that you heard this semester and reflect on the ways they changed your understanding of the topics discussed or the larger course topic. Write a memo in which you identify key ideas from your classmates' presentations that were most interesting, important, or provocative to you.

1. Identify the presentations you are going to discuss. Describe any commonalities you notice in the topics in your memo. Explain generally how these new perspectives are important to you.

2. Devote at least one paragraph to each presentation, focusing on the ideas your classmate(s) introduced that changed your way of thinking about the topic.

3. Explain how the classmate's presentation made you rethink your perspective.

4. Conclude by noting how you might apply these new perspectives in your current or future coursework, graduate school, or at work.

---

*Figure 8.1.* Reflection memo assignment.

Instructors also may use technology to facilitate the delivery of and response to student presentations and to widen the potential audience for student work. A number of respondents to the 2011 National Survey of Senior Capstone Experiences noted that student capstone projects resulted from collaborations with the local business community. For example, seniors in the School of Engineering at Fairfield University "sometimes partner with local industries to solve real-world problems," culminating in a presentation of their senior design projects (National Resource Center for The First-Year Experience & Students in Transition, 2011). Yet, a global economy means that today's *local* business may be in the next state or on another continent. Moreover, a compelling public health research question is as likely to emerge from conditions in another country as two counties away. Technology not only presents opportunities for students to gather information in support of their capstone projects at a distant, it also provides a vehicle for communicating their findings or proposed solution to an audience beyond the campus. To prepare future employees to communicate with remote audiences, Flatley (2007) had students make presentations in a business course using a virtual meeting management tool (e.g., Citrix's GoTo Meeting, Cisco's WebEx). As the globalization of industry continues, the need to make presentations to remote audiences will likely increase, as will the demand for employees who possess the skills to make them.

As noted above, instructors may be reluctant to devote too much class time to presentations—especially in larger classes. Similarly, if students are asked to evaluate their peers' presentations, they may become fatigued if the evaluations are all done within a short time frame. Chan (2011) recommended having students record their presentations using their own computers and then upload the video to a course management system or YouTube. Students can then review and respond to selected presentations. In addition to giving students greater confidence in working in multimedia, Chan found that recorded presentations "tend to be more creative than those done in class, and they can be more polished, as students will do repeated 'takes' to improve the quality of their presentations" (p. 75).

## Strategies for Helping Students Develop Oral Presentations

Smith and Sodano (2011) found that faculty may spend more time emphasizing the content of presentations than the oral communication skills needed to deliver them effectively. Still, students likely will need guidance on many issues as they prepare to make presentations for their peers or at department-sponsored conferences. Chan (2011) identified the following skill sets needed for oral presentations:

- planning, preparation, and development of visual aids, such as posters or PowerPoint presentations;

- identifying characteristics of strong and weak presentations;

- understanding and catering to audience needs;

- working effectively in groups;

- developing questions and offering critiques on others' work;

- responding to questions; and

- identifying and correcting ineffective delivery techniques related to body language, eye contact, tone, and pace.

To learn these skills, instructors could dedicate a class session to the topic or enlist staff at campus academic support centers to offer special workshops for students. Smith and Sodano (2011) found watching training videos was also an effective way to learn presentation skills. The remainder of this section takes a closer look at strategies for developing some of the skill sets identified by Chan, particularly analyzing audience, developing presentations, practicing delivery, and evaluating presentations.

### Identifying and Catering to Audience Needs

Speaking specifically of science education, Noblitt, Vance, and Smith (2010) suggested that scientists are increasingly called on to address public audiences and government entities, in face-to-face and broadcast settings, to explain their research and its broader implications (as cited in Chan, 2011). Indeed, because relatively few students ultimately will enter careers in academia, they will need experience describing the technical aspects of their field to an audience that has a more limited understanding of it. For this reason, skills in audience analysis are invaluable.

At the broadest level, audience analysis might involve exploring the audience's age, gender, education, cultural background, national and ethnic background, disposition toward the topic and the speaker, religious and political background, and socioeconomic status. However, such a detailed analysis may not be warranted for all speaking situations. The following questions can help guide students in thinking about their audience:

- Will those in the audience have an inherent interest in my subject? If not, how can I build that interest?

- What is my audience's knowledge about or experience with this topic likely to be?

- What values or beliefs are they likely to bring to this subject? How might this shape their reception to what I have to say?

- How familiar is my audience with my subject? What do I need to define, describe, and explain in order for them to fully understand my point?

- How is my take on this topic potentially controversial? How can I avoid alienating members of my audience as I present controversial interpretations or conclusions?

A careful audience analysis early in the planning process should drive the organization, development, and delivery of oral presentations, while avoiding gross overgeneralizations.

### *Developing Presentations*

As with a piece of formal writing, instructors will want to encourage students to make multiple drafts of a presentation. For panel presentations, students may write the complete speech, which may be a scaled-down version of their larger project paper. A good rule of thumb is to allow for one minute per page for delivering the paper at a good pace. In most cases, students will want a draft of no more than 10-12 pages for a 15-minute presentation slot with time for questions. Writing a full draft of a speech will help students incorporate plans from analyzing their audience and choosing ways to appeal to their listeners. It also will help them make audience-appropriate stylistic choices, such as integrating technical language followed by explanations or choosing precise wording rather than using slang or regional dialect expressions. Finally, having a full draft of the presentation or speech is useful for conferences with instructors, mentors, and classmates, who can provide greater clarity and depth in responding to its development.

The written version of the speech also can be the basis for a PowerPoint presentation or a poster, but students will need guidance on editing and designing their content for delivery in a largely visual medium. For PowerPoint, students should consider the

- size of type and readability of font,

- contrast between slide background and text,

- amount of text per slide,

- number of slides in the presentation (about one slide per minute),

- number and detail of graphic elements included on the slides, and

- inclusion of animation.

With poster sessions, students are constrained by the overall poster dimensions (e.g., 3x4 feet or 3x5 feet) and must make choices about font, type size, and kinds and number of graphic elements to include. The poster should also have a logical flow and visual structure to guide the reader through standard sections (e.g., introduction, abstract, method, results, implications for research and practice, references, and acknowledgements). A student at LSU in a peer review workshop intended to give students feedback on their poster designs offered this insight:

> Creating a poster and participating in a poster session ultimately solidifies your knowledge of your subject. The preparation forces you to look at your data in a novel way to predict audience responses to anticipate their questions. One of the problems with science is that the information is not always accessible to the common person, the CxC presentations and workshops made us aware that the poster design would influence the audience's response (because no one wants to look at a boring poster even if the scientific implications are profound). I have since given greater thought to the design elements when presenting my research so that my results will not be encumbered by awkward design. (Fava, 2009, Learning Goals section, para. 5)

Whether or not students develop a complete written draft of their presentation, instructors will want to offer some guidance on the basic outline and purpose of each section of the presentation, just as they would with a formal essay assignment. Figure 8.2 provides some general categories, which instructors can customize to the discipline and/or presentation type.

### Presentation Notes

Whether students are delivering a paper or making a presentation using PowerPoint, they will benefit from a set of working notes to refine and practice their delivery. They might use 3x5 cards, the notes function in PowerPoint, or some other system. Whatever system they choose, students will find that writing notes for presentations will help them synthesize and summarize key ideas and review the material to determine whether it is audience-ready. Brief notes highlighting key ideas, rather than complete sentences or paragraphs, serve as reminders and force students to rehearse as speakers, not readers. Physical notes cards can be easily reorganized if the presentation order does not seem to flow well. In PowerPoint's presenter view, the notes section can be used to remind students of

**Planning Worksheet for Oral Presentation**

***Purpose:*** Completing this worksheet will help you make plans for your oral presentation.

1. Introduction
   - How will you create a lively opening that will interest your listeners?
   - What is your main point or research question?
   - How will you preview your supporting ideas or findings to help your listener follow your presentation?
2. Organizing the body of the presentation
   - What are the primary sections of your presentation?
   - What is the purpose of each section?
   - What are the primary ideas or information you will communicate in each section?
   - What is the best strategy for communicating that information to audience members so that you maintain their focus and interest?
   - How will you acknowledge resources that you have drawn on to support your findings or conclusions?
3. Conclusion
   - How do your findings or conclusions relate to previous studies or the larger conversation surrounding this topic?
   - If offering a proposal, how will you inspire audience members to take action or adopt a particular position?

*Figure 8.2.* Guidelines for planning a presentation.

points they want to make for a particular slide, freeing them from the need to put too much text on each slide. Students will discover as they practice that they are learning their material more effectively by working from notes rather than from sheets of paper with messy strings of sentences or from outlines. To be effective, physical notecards or electronic note panels should contain only as much written material as students can read with a quick glance. Figure 8.3 provides guidelines for helping students develop useful notecards.

## *Practicing Delivery*

With notes completed, reviewed, and revised, students are ready to start practicing. They should practice individually to check their timing and then work with one or two partners to get feedback on delivery, including timing, pacing,

1. Before making your notes, review a draft of your presentation and list the key points and essential information that you want to be sure to include in your talk.

2. Transfer these key points to cards, with only one main idea per card. Make the writing highly visible by using large print or highlighting the words in a bright color.

3. Below the key point, list the phrases that will help you explain your key point.

4. At the bottom of each card, write a phrase that will help you transition to your next main idea.

5. Number your notecards at the top so they can be quickly reassembled.

*Figure 8.3.* Guidelines for creating notecards.

volume, and expression. Pairing international students with American English speakers will create richer experiences for everyone. Native English speakers will appreciate the response from international students regarding their explanations, speed of delivery, enunciation, and reliance on slang or dialect. International students will benefit from providing this help as well as receiving feedback about their fluency, volume, voice projection, and clarity.

If it is not feasible to rehearse before an audience, or if students desire additional practice, they may choose to use lecture capture technologies (e.g., vodcasting, podcasting) to record and review practice sessions. PowerPoint allows presenters to record narrations, which students can review for pacing, timing, and the use of too many fillers (e.g., um, like). Further, many laptops and smartphones come equipped with video recording capabilities, allowing students to evaluate their facial expressions and body language during a rehearsal. In an experimental study, Smith and Sodano (2011) compared the experiences of students who had reviewed their presentations captured on video to students who had not. Students who had the opportunity for review were more likely to express confidence in their ability to assess their presentation skills, to believe that their skills had improved, and to say they could apply what they learned to future presentations. Given the ubiquity of this technology, instructors should encourage students to use it in preparing for their presentations.

Whether students are working alone or in small groups, keeping a practice log (Figure 8.4) will help them assess their readiness to make their presentation and offer guidance on how to improve their delivery. The practice log also can become a piece of the student's self-assessment of the presentation.

**Name:**                          **Date:**
                                   **Start Time:**
                                   **End Time:**

**Practice method:**               **Audience members:**

- Audience
- Audio recording
- Video recording
- Rehearsal

**Feedback received from audience:**

**Goals for improving presentation:**

**Specific areas for practice:**

- *Focus.* Main idea is reiterated at several points in talk.
- *Explanations.* Adequate support is present.
- *Timing.* Speech is neither too long nor too short.
- *Pace.* Speed allows listeners to hear every word but is varied to hold interest.
- *Enunciation.* Articulation of each word is clear.
- *Eye contact.* Sufficient eye contact with a variety of audience members throughout the talk.
- *Relating to audience.* Use of examples, definitions, and references to other sources help audience relate to my ideas.

*Figure 8.4.* Practice log for oral presentation.

### *Evaluating Oral Presentations*

At the University of North Carolina at Greensboro, students are required to enroll in a designated number of writing- and speaking-intensive courses. To support the development of such courses, Richard (2008) created a comprehensive guide outlining assignment possibilities, providing model course descriptions, and offering strategies for responding to and evaluating assignments. In particular, she identified eight areas for evaluation drawn from criteria developed by the National Communication Association:

- topic (appropriate for audience and occasion, including time);
- thesis (clear and appropriate for the audience and occasion);

- supporting material (content and development of points, use of evidence);

- organization (use of organizational patterns, clear introduction and conclusion, transitions make it easy to follow);

- language (appropriate with no slang or jargon, vivid);

- vocal variety (pitch, rate, intensity);

- pronunciation, grammar, and articulation; and

- physical behaviors (eye contact, body movement, facial expression, gestures) (p. 56).

Many of these criteria highlight concerns about communicating with an audience, and keeping the assessment focus on the single rhetorical principle of meeting an audience's needs will help students hone their communication skills in a way that promotes transfer to new contexts. A portfolio of supporting written material (e.g., audience analysis worksheets, speech drafts, notecards, practice logs) can be reviewed to determine how prominently audience concerns figured in the development of the presentation. For example, if students' presentations go beyond the time limit, their practice or rehearsal logs may indicate that they did not adequately rehearse their speeches and time themselves. A disorganized presentation may result from an incomplete written draft, or a lack of coherence may be reflected in notecards that omit key points. Feedback on their texts can also help students understand the basic rhetorical principles underlying all effective communication, especially in meeting the audience's needs as listener or reader.

As noted earlier, instructors need to offer students feedback on a range of performance criteria. Reviewing a portfolio of supporting written documents can aid in the evaluation of the content of a presentation, but students are particularly interested in feedback related to their delivery (i.e., speaking clearly, loudly, and slowly enough or staying focused). As students assume new identities as professionals, they may be curious about how they sound and look when speaking (Jensen & Lamoureux, 1997). Research on assessment of oral presentations (Jensen & Lamoureux, 1997) reinforces the benefits of providing encouraging, positive, and personalized feedback, although students are most likely to find evaluations most useful when they refer to specific aspects of the delivery.

Peers also can be enlisted in offering constructive criticism during practice sessions or the final presentation. Even though seminar classes are typically small (12-15 students), asking students to provide a thoughtful response to each presentation may be overwhelming. To manage the evaluation load for students and ensure that each presenter gets a range of feedback, two or three students might be assigned to write an evaluative memo for each presentation (Figure 8.5). Brief questions and responses to presentations can also be part of a research journal or other collection of informal writing that students have been producing over the semester, allowing them to incorporate this information into their growing knowledge base. Such practices can train students to be thoughtful listeners and consumers of information and get them in the habit of formulating good questions in response to presentations—skills that will support them in a range of professional and civic settings after college graduation.

---

**Peer Evaluation of Presentation**

1. Write a memo to your classmate, responding to his or her presentation.
2. Identify what you found most interesting, inspiring, or surprising in the presentation.
3. State at least one question for your classmate.
4. Identify any material that you found problematic, difficult to understand, or troubling.
5. Explain how this presentation has changed your perspective on the subject. Identify possible topics for future study that might lead to additional perspectives.

---

*Figure 8.5.* Peer evaluation assignment for oral presentation.

## Connecting Multiple Literacy Skills

As stated in *Beliefs About the Teaching of Writing* (NCTE, 2004), "writing has a complex relationship to talk":

> speakers usually write notes and, regularly, scripts, and they often prepare visual materials that include texts and images. Writers often talk in order to rehearse the language and content that will go into what they write, and conversation often provides an impetus or occasion for writing. (Writing Has a Complex Relationship section, para. 1)

This volume has explored the opportunities for conversation among students and between students and faculty members to support the development and revision of writing assignments. Shaw (1999) suggested an oral presentation requirement may strengthen the final written product, in part, "because of input received during the presentation" (p. 155) and that the audience may have an influence on the quality. With most written assignments, the instructor might be the only audience (or, at least, the only audience the student believes matters). With a presentation, students are forced to think about how the material will be received by their peers and others. Heightened concerns about audience actually may strengthen the quality of arguments and the ways in which they are presented.

Oral presentations can be enhanced by emphasizing many of the same key strategies used for the writing assignments described in chapter 7: (a) developing a positive ethos or character, (b) answering the So What and Who Cares questions, (c) situating the argument in the context of or in response to a larger conversation, and (d) anticipating and responding to objectives. While Aristotle's rhetorical appeals are routinely taught in writing classes as strategies for analyzing and building arguments, they were originally conceived to support the development of speeches. Therefore, it seems logical to revisit these appeals as invention strategies for the development of oral presentations. A focus on rhetorical appeals—ethos, logos, and pathos—also emphasizes audience awareness, helping students make conscious choices about content selection, arrangement, and style (Fritz, 1984). Figure 8.6 offers a range of questions instructors can select from or adapt in helping students structure or revise oral presentations.

Finally, oral presentations provide students opportunities to build a repertoire of rhetorical skills that transcend printed texts. That is, they must consider the ways in which the design of PowerPoint presentations, posters, handouts, and other supplemental materials impact the audience's understanding and potential receptivity to their message.

**Introduction:**

1. What appeals (i.e., ethical, logical, and/or emotional) would best help get my audience's attention as I begin my speech?
2. What kind of information does my audience need to understand very quickly?
3. How can I communicate important facts or ideas early in my speech?

**Ethos:**

1. What type of character do I want to project in my speech so that my audience trusts my opinions, believes that my ideas are beneficial, and acknowledges my credibility?
2. How do I create this character through my choices of topics to discuss, details and stories to incorporate, and information from reliable sources?
3. How can I craft my character to appeal to a diverse audience?

**Logos:**

1. What appeals to logic are crucial to making my speech persuasive?
2. What kinds of information from external sources should I reference? Where is it most important to place that information?
3. How can I reference authorities on my topic to help develop my ethos while maintaining my own voice?
4. What assumptions might interfere with the audience accepting my arguments?

**Pathos:**

1. Will it be suitable to make appeals to emotion?
2. If so, what kinds of emotions are reasonable to arouse in my audience to make my speech persuasive?
3. How do I want to use stories as examples to arouse emotions?
4. Where in my speech will it be most effective to connect to my audience emotionally?
5. What pitfalls do I need to avoid in making appeals to pathos?
6. How can I avoid becoming overly emotional as I make appeals to pathos?
7. What sort of emotional appeals might be annoying or offensive to my audience?
8. How can I balance logical and emotional appeals?
9. Where might I overwhelm my listeners with too much information?

**Emphasis:**

1. Where do I emphasize my key points?

2. Where do I emphasize the most crucial information?

3. How might I adjust my emphasis to be more persuasive?

**Supporting materials:**

1. What information would be best communicated in another format (e.g., image, table, figure, audio file, video file)?

2. How might I structure a one-page handout that would highlight key points and facts and sources?

3. What audiovisual materials would help my listeners retain difficult or important information?

4. Where would it be most effective to place these materials in support of my argument?

**Conclusion:**

1. What key ideas do I want to return to, perhaps in the use of a brief anecdote or quotation?

2. What kind of action do I want to encourage my audience to take with respect to my topic?

*Figure 8.6.* Rhetorical strategies for shaping an oral presentation.

## Conclusion

Making presentations based on their major projects for the senior capstone or leading a class discussion are experiences students will draw on after graduation. Whether they are contributing an opinion at a school board meeting, making a pitch for a new project at work, or giving a talk at a conference as part of their graduate education, students will find they rely on the same basic rhetorical principles they used to solve problems as writers when they organize, rehearse, revise, and reflect on their speeches. Writing activities that accompany the development of oral presentations—such as audience analyses, notes, and practice logs—will enhance students' speeches and their overall performance as communicators. Students may not revisit all of these activities each time they are called on to address an audience in the future, but the habits of mind such practices instill will undoubtedly inform all future performances.

# Conclusion

## Writing in the Senior Capstone:
## Recommendations for Successful Practice

Teaching always involves a great deal of hope and faith that what instructors do in the classroom will matter to students later in their lives, in ways that cannot always be imagined. When instructors receive feedback from former students who relate how a class helped them navigate some future challenge or stayed with them long after grades were posted, it affirms the value of the educational enterprise. As noted elsewhere, prominent goals for the senior capstone are to improve students' critical-thinking skills, foster scholarly research, prepare them for future careers, and enhance their proficiency in oral and written communication. Feedback from a graduate of IUP suggests that participation in a senior seminar helped him achieve many of these objectives. In particular, learning to focus his thinking when writing helped him put ideas into a framework and create manageable steps to accomplish tasks. Beyond these expected outcomes, the student also suggested the course instilled a lifelong love of writing:

> I love to write and keep a journal. I reflect quite often on my life and where it's going. I like to set goals for myself and check back in to see how I'm doing once in a while (R. Long, personal communication, January 29, 2013).

While not all students walk away from writing-intensive capstone experiences with a love of writing, perhaps they, like this student, will discover the value of writing as a powerful self-reflection tool. The senior capstone also can be an incubator for important civic values and dispositions, as this former student, who credits his seminar for his expanded commitment to conservation efforts, noted:

> Being able to have and use these areas is wonderful, and keeping them clean and natural through conservation has become very important to

me. I strongly support efforts that are intended to preserve our natural wild areas. I know I would not feel as strongly about conservation if I hadn't taken [the seminar] about the culture and history of our national parks. (J. Rice, personal communication, February 5, 2013)

Further, the practice in some capstones of actively engaging students in the selection of reading materials and writing topics can have a profound impact and help students synthesize their college learning and apply it to real-world situations.

In college or school a student may be forced to read/write on a subject to (obviously) learn about that subject, but after being able to read/ write about something that I enjoyed, I was able to apply that to how I select influences in my life today. (J. Rice, personal communication, February 5, 2013)

These kinds of reflections and observations illustrate the powerful potential for the capstone experience to spur intellectual, professional, and personal development long after graduation. As the first part of this book argues, writing is a potent facilitator of development along these lines.

To that end, this volume concludes by revisiting the theory and practice discussed earlier with the goal of helping instructors make more effective use of writing as a tool for learning and personal and professional development in the senior capstone. Here, some final recommendations for incorporating manageable and rewarding writing assignments and processes in capstones are offered.

To ensure that writing assignments lead to positive student learning outcomes, faculty should

- teach the writing process as problem solving,
- include informal writing throughout the course,
- provide occasions for students to reflect on their learning,
- balance collaboration with independent work,
- incorporate a portfolio approach to help students synthesize and integrate information and experiences, and
- connect the development of writing skills to that of professional identity.

As noted earlier, writing is a powerful tool for learning, and it has the potential to facilitate advanced reasoning skills when students are engaged in challenging assignments. To promote students' intellectual development through the assignment of writing, instructors can

- use sequenced writing activities and ill-structured problems to help students move toward greater cognitive complexity,
- provide appropriate scaffolding and support when challenging students to develop advanced critical-thinking levels,
- create research problems that require students to evaluate sources from different perspectives, and
- design writing and discussion activities that help students develop original and creative thinking.

The development of written and oral communication skills is critical for the successful transition to work or graduate school. To ensure that students are well prepared to make this transition, capstone experiences should

- integrate oral and written communication activities,
- include genres (e.g., memos, proposals, reports, summaries) to help students translate academic writing into workplace writing, and
- embed electronic communications into writing assignments.

Once faculty have made the commitment to incorporate writing into the seminar, they will want to ensure that it is indeed helping students achieve course learning outcomes and, in many cases, the outcomes desired by the major, department, and institution. Well-designed and thoughtful assessment practices not only provide faculty with insight into how writing is working in their courses, but they also have the potential to deepen the learning experience for students. Yet, many faculty may resist assessment, fearing that it will be onerous and disconnected from their goals for students. Assessment practices can become more manageable and meaningful when faculty base the process on factors related to general course goals and

- evaluate writing selectively, rather than trying to assess all features simultaneously or all writing that students produce in a course;
- include self-assessment throughout the writing process; and
- work with students, colleagues, and administrators to incorporate portfolio assessment at the course, departmental, and programmatic levels.

In the coming years, senior capstones will have to adapt to educational, social, and economic pressures. As institutions face budget changes, they may choose to increase class sizes, which can affect instructors' workload and, thus, the curricula of their courses. Adding writing projects when a course already seems complete, or when there are suddenly five more students enrolled, can seem to be more of a problematic than effective pedagogy. However, as this book presents, there are ways to make writing assignments manageable so that instructors do not feel overworked, especially when they are willing to give students a role in assessment. When budget constraints drive curriculum reform, meeting students' needs and strengthening learning will still be a priority. Morever, reform efforts can lead to creative and innovative practices that benefit students and faculty.

Portfolios, culminating projects, or senior theses are invaluable to students as they prepare for the next phase of their lives. As they leave their academic homes after graduation and enter the workforce, graduate school, and their communities, they will carry with them a document that illustrates their achievements, development, and strengths as learners and thinkers. Their writing will remain with them to remind them of what they have accomplished as well as what they will be capable of in the future. In their major writing projects, theses, or portfolios, students will see evidence of their beliefs, values, dreams, and skills and know they can face new challenges and contexts in which all forms of communication will always be important.

# References

Abes, E. S., Jones, S. R., & McEwen, M. K. (2007). Reconceptualizing the model of multiple dimensions of identity: The role of meaning-making capacity in the construction of multiple identities. *Journal of College Student Development, 48*(1), 1-22.

Addison, J., & McGee, S. J. (2010). Writing in high school/writing in college: Research trends and future directions. *College Composition and Communication, 62*(1), 147-180.

Allen, M. J. (2006). *Assessing general education programs.* San Francisco, CA: Anker.

Annis, L., & Jones, C. (1995). Student portfolios: Their objectives, development, and use. In P. Seldin & Associates (Eds.), *Improving college teaching* (p. 188). Boston, MA: Anker Publishing.

Aristotle. (1991). *Rhetoric* (G. Kennedy, Trans.). New York, NY: Oxford University Press.

Assaf, L. C., Ash, G. E., Saunders, J., & Johnson, J. (2011). Renewing two seminal literacy practices: I-Charts and I-Search papers. *Voices From the Middle, 18*(4), 31-42.

Association of American Colleges. (1985). *Integrity in the college curriculum: A report to the academic community.* Washington, DC: Author.

Association of American Colleges and Universities (AAC&U). (2004). *Our students' best work: A framework for accountability worthy of our mission.* Washington, DC: Author. Retrieved from http://www.aacu.org/publications/pdfs/StudentsBestreport.pdf

Association of American Colleges and Universities. (2007). *College learning for the new global century.* Washington, DC: Author. Retrieved from http://www.aacu.org/leap/documents/GlobalCentury_final.pdf

Baker, M. P. (1997). *"What is English?" Developing a senior "capstone" course for the English major.* Retrieved from ERIC database. (ED411512)

Barefoot, B. O., Griffin, B. Q., & Koch, A. (2012). *Enhancing student success and retention throughout undergraduate education: A national survey.* Brevard, NC: John N. Gardner Institute for Excellence in Undergraduate Education.

Baxter Magolda, M. (1992). *Knowing and reasoning in college: Gender-related patterns in students' intellectual development.* San Francisco, CA: Jossey-Bass.

Baxter Magolda, M. (1999). *Creating contexts for learning and self-authorship. Constructive-developmental pedagogy.* Nashville, TN: Vanderbilt University Press.

Baxter Magolda, M. (2001). *Making their own way: Narratives for transforming higher education to promote self-development.* Sterling, VA: Stylus.

Baxter Magolda, M., & King, P. M. (2004). *Learning partnerships: Theory and models of practice to educate for self-authorship.* Sterling, VA: Stylus.

Bazerman, C. (2009). Genre and cognitive development: Beyond writing to learn. In C. Bazerman, A. Bonini, & D. Fiqueiredo (Eds.), *Genre in a changing world: Perspectives on writing* (pp. 279-294). West Lafayette, IN: Parlor Press. Retrieved from http://wac.colostate.edu/books/genre. 01/28/2013

Beach, R., & Doerr-Stevens, C. (2009). Learning argument practices through online role-play: Toward a rhetoric of significance and transformation. *Journal of Adolescent & Adult Literacy. 52*(6), 460-468. doi:10.1598/JAAL.52.6.1

Bean, J. (2011). *Engaging ideas: The professor's guide to integrating writing, critical thinking, and active learning in the classroom* (2nd ed.). San Francisco, CA: Jossey-Bass.

Berrett, D. (2012, July 30). College too easy? UCLA makes it tougher. *The Chronicle of Higher Education*, pp. A1, A10-11.

Box, J. A., & Dean, C. D. (1995). Professional portfolio process. In T. W. Banta, J. P. Lund, K. E. Black, & F. W. Oblander (Eds.), *Assessment in practice: Putting principles to work on college campuses* (pp. 113-115). San Francisco, CA: Jossey-Bass.

Boyer Commission on Educating Undergraduates in the Research University. (1998). *Reinventing undergraduate education: A blueprint for America's research universities.* Retrieved from http://naples.cc.sunysb.edu/Pres/boyer.nsf

Boyer Commission on Educating Undergraduates in the Research University. (2001). *Reinventing undergraduate education: Three years after the Boyer Report.* Retrieved from https://dspace.sunyconnect.suny.edu/bitstream/1951/26013/1/Reinventing%20Undergraduate%20Education%20(Boyer%20Report%20II).pdf)

Brent, D. (2012). Crossing boundaries: Co-op students relearning to write. *College Composition and Communication, 63*(4), 558-592.

Bresciani, M. J., Zelna, C. L., & Anderson, J. A. (2004). *Assessing student learning and development: A handbook for practitioners.* Washington, DC: National Association of Student Personnel Administrators.

Bressoud, D. M. (1999). The one-minute paper. In B. Gold, S. Z. Keith, & W. A. Marion (Eds.), *Assessment practices in undergraduate mathematics* (pp. 87-88). Washington, DC: The Mathematical Association of America.

Brookfield, S. D. (2011). *Teaching for critical thinking: Tools and techniques to help students question their assumptions.* San Francisco, CA: Jossey-Bass.

Cardillo, F. M., & Koritz, H. G. (1979). A new approach to senior seminar. *Journal of College Science Teaching, 8*(5), 295-297.

Carlson, C. D., & Peterson, R. J. (1993). Social problems and policy: A capstone course. *Teaching Sociology, 21*, 239-241.

Chan, V. (2011). Teaching oral communication in undergraduate science: Are we doing enough and doing it right? *Journal of Learning Design, 4*(3), 71-79.

Chew, E. B., McInnis-Bowers, C., Cleveland, P. A., & Drewer, L. A. (1996). The business administration capstone: Assessment and integrative learning. *Liberal Education, 82*(1), 44-49. Retrieved from http://web.ebscohost.com

Chickering, A. W., & Reisser, L. (1993). *Education and identity* (2nd ed.). San Francisco, CA: Jossey-Bass.

Collier, P. J. (2000). The effects of completing a capstone course on student identity. *Sociology of Education, 73*(4), 285-299.

Condon, W. (2011). Review essay: Reinventing writing assessment: How the conversation is shifting. *Writing Program Administration, 34*(2), 162-182.

Conference Board, Corporate Voices for Working Families, the Partnership for 21st Century Skills, & the Society for Human Resource Management. (2006). *Are they really ready to work? Employers' perspectives on the basic knowledge and applied skills of new entrants to the 21st century U.S. workforce.* Retrieved from http://www.p21.org/documents/FINAL_REPORT_PDF09-29-06.pdf

Conference on College Composition and Communication (CCCC) Committee on Assessment. (2006, revised 2009). *Writing assessment: A position statement.* Urbana, Illinois: NCTE. Retrieved from http://www.ncte.org/cccc/resources/positions/writingassessment

Conference on College Composition and Communication (CCCC) Taskforce on Best Practices in Electronic Portfolios (2007, November). *Principles and practices in electronic portfolios.* Retrieved from www.ncte.org/cccc/resources/positions/electronic-portfolios

Council of Writing Program Administrators. (2011). *Framework for success in postsecondary writing.* Retrieved from http://wpacouncil.org/files/framework-for-success-post-secondary-writing.pdf

Danielewicz, J. (2008). Personal genres, public voices. *College Composition and Communication, 59*(3), 420-450.

Davis, R., & Shadle, M. (2000). Building a mystery: Alternative research writing and the academic act of seeking. *College Composition and Communication, 51*(3), 417-446.

Devitt, A. J. (2000). Integrating rhetorical and literary theories of genre. *College English, 62*(6), 696-718.

Doerr-Stevens, C., Beach, R., & Boeser, E. (2011). Using online role-play to promote collaborative argument and collective action. *English Journal, 100*(5), 33-39.

Dunlap, J. C. (2005). Problem-based learning and self-efficacy: How a capstone course prepares students for a profession. *Educational Technology Research and Development, 53*(1), 65-85.

Durel, R. J. (1993). The capstone course: A rite of passage. *Teaching Sociology, 21*, 223-225.

Elbow, P. (1987). Closing my eyes as I speak: An argument for ignoring audience. *College English, 49*(1), 50-69.

Elbow, P. (1991). Toward a phenomenology of freewriting. In P. Belanoff, P. Elbow, & S. I. Fontaine (Eds.), *Nothing begins with N: New investigations of freewriting* (pp. 113-136). Originally published in *Basic Writing* (1989), *8*(2), 44-71. Carbondale & Edwardsville, IL: Southern Illinois University Press.

Elbow, P. (1998). *Writing without teachers* (2nd ed.). New York, NY: Oxford.

Ellings, R. J., Rush, K., & Cushman, A. H. (1989). Task force: A senior seminar for undergraduate majors in international studies. *Political Science Teacher, 2*(1), 6-7.

English, L. M. (2001). Ethical concerns relating to journal writing. In L. M. English & M. A. Gillen (Eds.), *Promoting journal writing in adult education* (New Directions for Adult and Continuing Education, No. 90, pp. 27-35). San Francisco, CA: Jossey-Bass.

Ervin, E. (1998). English 496: Senior seminar in writing: "Writing for Diverse Publics." *Composition Studies Freshman English News, 26*(1), 37-57.

Fava, C. H. (2009). *Developing professional communication skills in an undergraduate research experience poster session.* Retrieved from the Pedagogy in Action website: http://serc.carleton.edu/sp/library/communications_curricula/examples/example5.html

Fava, C. H., & Mangiavellano, D. (n.d.). *Poster project description.* Baton Rouge, LA: Louisiana State University, College of Basic Sciences. Retrieved from the Pedagogy in Action website: http://serc.carleton.edu/sp/library/communications_curricula/examples/example5.html

Fenwick, T. J. (2001). Responding to journals in a learning process. In L. M. English & M. A. Gillen (Eds.), *Promoting journal writing in adult education* (New Directions for Adult and Continuing Education No. 90, pp. 37-47). San Francisco, CA: Jossey-Bass.

Field, P. (2005). Creating case study presentations: A survey of senior seminar students. *Journal of College Science Teaching, 35*(1), 56-59.

Fischer, B. A., & Zigmond, M. J. (1998). Survival skills for graduate school and beyond. *New Directions for Higher Education, 101,* 29-40.

Flatley, M. E. (2007). Teaching the virtual presentation. *Business Communication Quarterly, 70*(3), 301-305.

Fleron, J. F., & Hotchkiss, P. K. (2001). First-year and senior seminars: Dual seminars = stronger mathematics majors. *Primus, 11*(4), 289-324.

Foubert, J. D., Nixon, M. L., Sisson, V. S., & Barnes, A. C. (2005). A longitudinal study of Chickering and Reisser's vectors: Exploring gender differences and implications for refining the theory. *Journal of College Student Development, 46*(5), 461-471.

Frantz, D. A. (1999). Using a capstone course to assess a variety of skills. In B. Gold, S. Z. Keith, & W. A. Marion (Eds.), *Assessment practices in undergraduate mathematics* (pp. 31-34). Washington, DC: The Mathematical Association of America.

Fritz, P. A (1984, November). *Teaching critical thinking skills in the public speaking course: A liberal arts perspective.* Paper presented at the 70th Annual Meeting of the Speech Communication Association, Chicago, IL. (ERIC Document Reproduction Service No. ED248556).

Fulwiler, T., & Jones, R. (1982). Assigning and evaluating transactional writing. In T. Fulwiler & A. Young (Eds.), *Language connections: Writing and reading across the curriculum* (pp. 45-55). Urbana, IL: NCTE. Retrieved from the WAC Clearinghouse website: http://wac.colostate.edu/books/language_connections/

Gere, A. R., Aull, L, Dickinson, H., Gerben, C., Green, T., Moody, E., Moody, S., McBee Orzulak, M., & Thomas, E. T. (2008). *Writing now: A policy research brief.* Urbana, IL: NCTE. Retrieved from http://www.ncte.org/library/NCTEFiles/Resources/PolicyResearch/WrtgResearchBrief.pdf

Gillis, A. J. (2001). Journal writing in health education. In L. M. English & M. A. Gillen (Eds.), *Promoting journal writing in adult education* (New Directions for Adult and Continuing Education, No. 90, pp. 49-58). San Francisco, CA: Jossey-Bass.

Graff, G., & Birkenstein, C. (2010). *They say/I say: The moves that matter in academic writing* (2nd ed.). New York, NY: W. W. Norton.

Hall, A. (2012, November). *Public relations students gain real life experience from writing class.* Retrieved from the School of Journalism and Mass Communications, University of South Carolina web site: http://jour.sc.edu/news/newsann/12Fall/mckeever_class.html

Hammond, L. (1991). Using focused freewriting to promote critical thinking. In P. Belanoff, P. Elbow, & S. I. Fontaine (Eds.), *Nothing begins with N: New investigations of freewriting* (pp. 71-92). Carbondale & Edwardsville, IL: Southern Illinois University Press.

Hart Research Associates. (2010). *Raising the bar: Employers' views on college learning in the wake of the economic downturn.* Washington, DC: Association of American Colleges and Universities. Retrieved from the AAC&U website: http://www.aacu.org/leap/public_opinion_research.cfm

Hart Research Associates. (2013). *It takes more than a major: Employer priorities for college learning and student success.* Washington, DC: Association of American Colleges and Universities. Retrieved from the AAC&U website: http://www.aacu.org/leap/documents/2013_EmployerSurvey.pdf

Hathaway, D. K., & Atkinson, D. (2001). The senior seminar: Preparation for life after college. *Primus, 11*(4), 326-36.

Hauhart, R. C., & Grahe, J. E. (2010). The undergraduate capstone course in the social sciences: Results from a regional survey. *Teaching Sociology, 38*(1), 4-17.

Hawke, S. D. (1983). Liberal arts and the biology seminar experience. *Journal of College Science Teaching, 13*(2), 88-90,128.

Hays, J. N. (1995). Intellectual parenting and a developmental feminist pedagogy of writing. In J. Emig & L. W. Phelps (Eds.), *Feminine principles and women's experience in American composition and rhetoric* (pp. 153-190). Pittsburgh, PA: University of Pittsburgh Press.

Hays, J. N., Brandt, K. M., & Chantry, K. H. (1988). The impact of friendly and hostile audiences on argumentative writing of high school and college students. *Research in the Teaching of English, 22*(4), 391-416.

Henscheid, J. M. (2000). *Professing the disciplines: An analysis of senior seminars and capstone courses* (Monograph No. 30). Columbia, SC: University of South Carolina, National Research Center for The First-Year Experience & Students in Transition.

Henscheid, J. M. (2008, November/December). Preparing seniors for life after college. *About Campus,* 20-25.

Hiemstra, R. (2001). Uses and benefits of journal writing. In L. M. English & M. A. Gillen (Eds.), *Promoting journal writing in adult education* (New Directions for Adult and Continuing Education, No. 90, pp. 19-26). San Francisco, CA: Jossey-Bass.

Hodges, E. (1997). Negotiating the margins: Some principles for responding to our students' writing, some strategies for helping students read our comments. *New Directions for Teaching and Learning, 69*, 77-89.

Hummer, A. (1997, May-June). Measuring critical thinking outcomes via the capstone course paper. *Assessment Update, 9*(3), 8-9.

Huot, B. (2002). *(Re)Articulating writing assessment for teaching and learning.* Logan, UT: Utah State University Press.

Huyett, P. (1996). Stimulating faculty interest in portfolio assessment. In T. W. Banta, J. P. Lund, K. E. Black, & F. W. Oblander (Eds.), *Assessment in practice: Putting principles to work on college campuses* (pp. 306-308). San Francisco, CA: Jossey-Bass.

Jensen, K., & Lamoureux, E. R. (1997). Written feedback in the basic course: What instructors provide and what students deem helpful. In L. Hugenberg (Ed.), *Basic communication course annual* (pp. 37-58). Boston, MA: American Press.

Jolliffe, D. A. (2001). Writing across the curriculum and service learning: Kairos, genre, and collaboration. In S. McLeod, E. Miraglia, M. Soven, & C. Thaiss (Eds.), *Writing across the curriculum for the new millennium: Strategies for continuing writing across the curriculum programs* (pp. 86-108). Urbana, IL: National Council of Teachers of English.

Jones, C. G. (1996). The portfolio as a course assessment tool. In T. W. Banta, J. P. Lund, K. E. Black, & F. W. Oblander (Eds.), *Assessment in practice: Putting principles to work on college campuses* (pp. 285-288). San Francisco, CA: Jossey-Bass.

Jones, S. R., & McEwen, M. K. (2000). A conceptual model of multiple dimensions of identity. *Journal of College Student Development, 41*(4), 405-414.

Kalivas, J. H. (2008). A service-learning project based on a research supportive curriculum format in the general chemistry laboratory. *Journal of Chemistry Education, 85*(10), 1410-1415.

King, P. M., & Kitchener, K. S. (1994). *Developing reflective judgment: Understanding and promoting intellectual growth and critical thinking adolescents and adults.* San Francisco, CA: Jossey-Bass.

King, P. M., & Kitchener, K. S. (2002). The reflective judgment model: Twenty years of research on epistemic cognition. In B. K. Hofer & P. R. Pinrich (Eds.), *Personal epistemology: The psychology of beliefs about knowledge and knowing* (pp. 37-61). Mahwah, NJ: Lawrence Erlbaum Associates.

King, P. M., & Kitchener, K. S. (2004). Reflective judgment: Theory and research on the development of epistemic assumptions through adulthood. *Educational Psychologist, 39*(1), 5-18.

Klausman, J. (2007). Resurrecting the I-Search: Engaging students in meaningful scholarship. *Teaching English in the Two-Year College, 35*(2), 191-196.

Kroll, B. M. (1992). *Teaching hearts and minds: College students reflect on the Vietnam War in literature.* Carbondale, IL: Southern Illinois University Press.

Kuh, G. D. (2008). *High-impact educational practices: What they are, who has access to them, and why they matter.* Washington, DC: Association of American Colleges and Universities.

Lamb, C. E. (1991). Beyond argument in feminist composition. *College Composition and Communication, 42*(1), 11-24.

Leskes, A., & Miller, R. (2006). *Purposeful pathways: Helping students achieve key learning outcomes.* Washington, DC: Association of American Colleges and Universities.

Lyman, H. (2006). I-Search in the age of information. *English Journal, 95*(4), 62-67.

Lynch, D. A., George, D., & Cooper, M. M. (1997). Moments of argument: Agonistic inquiry and confrontational cooperation. *College Composition and Communication, 48*(1), 61-85.

Macrorie, K. (1988). *The I-search paper* (Revised edition of *Searching writing*). Portsmouth, NH: Boyton/Cook.

Mayfield, B. (2001). A history of mathematics course as a senior seminar. *Primus, 11*(3), 245-257.

McElroy, J. L. (1997). The mentor demonstration model: Writing with students in the senior economics seminar. *Journal of Economic Education, 28*(1), 31-35.

McGoldrick, K. (2008). Writing requirements and economic research opportunities in the undergraduate curriculum: Results from a survey of departmental practices. *Journal of Economic Education, 39*(3), 287-296.

McKee, K., & Pistole, D. (2010). *University assessment—liberal studies subcommittee. Summary report of the local assessment of IUP's expected learning outcomes for the academic year 2009-2010.* Retrieved from www.iup.edu/WorkArea/DownloadAsset.aspx?id=104719

McLeod, C. (Producer and Director), & Maynor, M. (Coproducer). (2001). *In the light of reverence [Motion picture].* USA: Bullfrog Films.

Meltzer, D. (2009). Writing assignments across the curriculum: A national study of college writing. *College Composition and Communication, 61*(2), 240-261.

Miller, C. R. (1994). Rhetorical community: The cultural basis of genre. In A. Freedman & P. Medway (Eds.), *Genre and the new rhetoric* (pp. 67-78). London and Bristol, PA: Taylor and Francis Publishing.

Miller, C. R., & Shepherd, D. (2004). Blogging as social action: A genre analysis of the weblog. In L. J. Gurak, S. Antonijevic, L. Johnson, C. Ratliff, & J. Reyman (Eds.), *Into the blogosphere: Rhetoric, community, and culture of weblogs.* Retrieved from http://blog.lib.umn.edu/blogosphere/blogging_as_social_action.html

Moore, C., O'Neill, P., & Huot, B. (2009). Creating a culture of assessment in writing programs and beyond. *College Composition and Communication, 61*(1), 107-133.

Mullen, C. (2006). Best writing practices for graduate students: Reducing the discomfort of the blank screen. *Kappa Delta Pi Record, 43*(1), 30-35.

National Association of Colleges and Employers (NACE). (2009). *Job outlook 2010.* Bethlehem, PA: Author. Retrieved from http: www.naceweb.org

National Commission on Writing. (2004). *Writing: A ticket to work … or a ticket out: A survey of business leaders.* Retrieved from http://www.collegeboard.com/prod_downloads/writingcom/writing-ticket-to-work.pdf

National Council of Teachers of English (NCTE) Executive Committee. (2004). *Beliefs about the teaching of writing*. Urban, IL: Author. Retrieved from http://www.ncte.org/positions/statements/writingbeliefs

National Resource Center for The First-Year Experience & Students in Transition. (2011). *National Survey of Senior Capstone Experiences*. Unpublished raw data.

Ostheimer, M. W., & White, E. M. (2005). Portfolio assessment in an American engineering college. *Assessing Writing, 10*(1), 61-73.

Padgett, R. D., & Kilgo, C. A. (2012). *2011 National Survey of Senior Capstone Experiences: Institution-level data on the culminating experience* (Research Reports on College Transitions No. 3). Columbia, SC: University of South Carolina, National Resource Center for The First-Year Experience & Students in Transition.

Palomba, C. A., & Banta, T. W. (1999). *Assessment essentials: Planning, implementing, and improving assessment in higher education*. San Francisco, CA: Jossey-Bass.

Pegram, D. M. (2006). What If? Teaching research and creative-thinking skills through proposal writing. *English Journal, 95*(4), 17-21.

Perry, W. (1999). *Forms of intellectual and ethical development in the college years: A scheme*. San Francisco, CA: Jossey-Bass. (Original work published 1968)

Peterson, S. M., Phillips, A., Bacon, S. I., & Machunda, Z. (2011). Teaching evidence-based practice at the BSW level: An effective capstone project. *Journal of Social Work Education, 47*(3), 509-524.

Rafoth, B. (1988). Discourse community: Where writers, readers, and texts come together. In B. Rafoth & D. A. Rubin (Eds.), *The social construction of written communication* (pp. 131-146). Norwood, NY: Ablex.

Reave, L. (2002). Promoting innovation in the workplace: The internal proposal. *Business Communication Quarterly, 65*(4), 8-21.

Rex, L. A., Thomas, E. E., & Engel, S. (2010). Applying Toulmin: Teaching logical reasoning and argumentative writing. *English Journal, 99*(6), 56-63.

Reynolds, N., & Rice, R. (2006). *Portfolio teaching: A guide for instructors* (2nd ed.). Boston, MA: Bedford/St. Martin's.

Rhodes, T. L. (Ed.). (2010). *Assessing outcomes and improving achievements: Tips and tools for using rubrics*. Washington, DC: Association of American Colleges and Universities.

Rhodes, T. L., & Agre-Kippenhan, S. (2004). A multiplicity of learning: Capstones at Portland State University. *Assessment Update, 16*(4), 4-12.

Richard, M. J. (Ed.). (2008). *Communication across the curriculum. A faculty guide to teaching writing intensive and speaking intensive courses* (3rd ed.). Greensboro, NC: University of North Carolina at Greensboro. Retrieved from http://www.uncg.edu/cac/faculty_resources/guide.html

Russell, D. R. (2001). Where do the naturalistic studies of WAC/WID point? A research review. In S. McLeod, E. Miraglia, M. Soven, & C. Thaiss (Eds.), *Writing across the curriculum for the new millennium: Strategies for continuing writing across the curriculum programs* (pp. 259-298). Urbana, IL: National Council of Teachers of English.

Ruszkiewicz, J., Friend, C., & Hairston, M. (2008). *Scott Foresman Handbook, Compact* (2nd ed.). Upper Saddle River, NJ: Pearson Education.

Schmid, T. J. (1993). Bringing sociology to life: The other capstone mandate. *Teaching Sociology, 21,* 219-222.

Schneider, C. G. (2008). Liberal education and high-impact practices: Making excellence—once and for all—inclusive. In G. D. Kuh (Ed.), *High-impact educational practices: What they are, who has access to them, and why they matter* (pp. 1-8). Washington, DC: Association of American Colleges and Universities.

Seeborg, M. C. (2008). Achieving proficiencies in economics capstone courses. *Journal of College Teaching & Learning, 5*(2), 61-74.

Shaw, V. N. (1999). Reading, presentation, and writing skills in content courses. *College Teaching, 47*(4), 153-157.

Simmons, J. (2003). Responders are taught, not born. *Journal of Adolescent & Adult Literacy, 46*(8), 684-693.

Sitler, H. C. (1993). What college writing instructors expect and why you should join the resistance. *English Journal, 82*(6), 21-25.

Skipper, T. L. (2009). *Connecting cognitive-structural development and writing performance: Implications for the first-year composition classroom* (Unpublished doctoral dissertation). University of South Carolina, Columbia, SC.

Smith, C. M., & Sodano, T. M. (2011). Integrating lecture capture as a teaching strategy to improve student presentation skills through self-assessment. *Active Learning in Higher Education, 12*(3), 151-162.

Smith, L. S., & Crowther, E. H. (1996). Portfolios: Useful tools for assessment in business technology. In T. W. Banta, J. P. Lund, K. E. Black, & F. W. Oblander (Eds.), *Assessment in practice: Putting principles to work on college campuses* (pp. 115-117). San Francisco, CA: Jossey-Bass.

Smith, W. L. (1993). The capstone course at Loras College. *Teaching Sociology, 21,* 250-252.

Sommers, N. (2006). Across the drafts in rethinking Nancy Sommers's "Responding to Student Writing." *College Composition and Communication, 58*(2), 246-267.

Stephens, R. P., Jones, K. W., & Barrow, M. V. (2011). The book project: Engaging history majors in undergraduate research. *The History Teacher, 45*(1), 65-80.

Strickland, J. (2004). Just the FAQs: An alternative to teaching the research paper. *English Journal, 94*(1), 23-28.

Sullivan, K. (2009). *Building professional communication skills in microbiology.* Retrieved from the Pedagogy in Action website: http://serc.carleton.edu/sp/library/communications_curricula/examples/example3.htm

Sullivan, B. F., & Thomas, S. L. (2007). Documenting student learning outcomes through a research-intensive senior capstone experience: Bringing the data together to demonstrate progress. *North American Journal of Psychology, 9*(2), 321-330.

Thaiss, C., & Zawacki, T. M. (2006). *Engaged writers: Dynamic disciplines: Research on the academic writing life.* Portsmouth, NH: Boynton Cook/Heinemann.

Tinto, V. (1993). *Leaving college: Rethinking the causes and cures of student attrition* (2nd ed.). Chicago, IL: University of Chicago Press.

Trebay, G. (2012, November 28). Guess who isn't coming to dinner. *The New York Times.* Retrieved from http://www.nytimes.com/2012/11/29/fashion/saving-the-endangered-dinner-party.html

Troyer, R. J. (1993). Comments on the capstone course. *Teaching Sociology, 21*, 246-249.

Veerman, A., Andriessen, J., & Kanselaar, G. (2002). Collaborative argumentation in academic education. *Instructional Science, 30*, 155-186.

Wagenaar, T. C. (1993). The capstone course. *Teaching Sociology, 21*, 209-214.

Wallner, A. S., & Latosi-Sawin, E. (1999). Technical writing and communication in a senior-level chemistry seminar. *Journal of Chemical Education, 76*(10), 1404-1406.

Walvoord, B., & McCarthy, L. P. (1990). *Thinking and writing in college: A naturalistic study of students in four disciplines.* Urbana, IL: NCTE.

Wei, K., Siow, J., & Burley, D. L. (2007). Implementing service-learning to the information systems and technology management program: A study of an undergraduate capstone course. *Journal of Information Systems Education, 18*(1), 125-136.

White, A. (1999). Journals: Assessment without anxiety. In B. Gold, S. Z. Keith, & W. A. Marion (Eds.), *Assessment practices in undergraduate mathematics* (pp. 129-130). Washington, DC: The Mathematical Association of America.

Williams, D. E., & McGee, B. R. (2000). Negotiating change in the argumentation course. *Teaching cooperative argument, 3*, 105-119.

Worthy, S. L., Taylor, J. C., & Cheek, W. K. (2008). Mississippi State undergrad program teaches grant writing. *Journal of Family and Consumer Sciences, 100*(4), 51-52.

Yagelski, R. P. (2009). A thousand writers writing: Seeking change through the radical practice of writing as a way of being. *English Education, 42*(1), 6-28.

Young, R. E. (2011). *Toward a taxonomy of "small" genres and writing techniques for use in writing across the curriculum.* Fort Collins, CO: The WAC Clearinghouse. Retrieved from http://wac.colostate.edu/books/young/

Zechmeister, E. B., & Reich, J. N. (1994). Teaching undergraduates about teaching undergraduates: A capstone course. *Teaching of Psychology, 21*(1), 24-28.

# Index

NOTE: Page numbers with italicized *f*, *t*, and *n* indicate figures, tables, or footnotes respectively.

# About
# the Authors

**Lea Masiello** is professor emeritus, Department of English, Indiana University of Pennsylvania (IUP), where she taught for 26 years. She earned her BA, MA, and PhD at The University of Cincinnati, concentrating on rhetoric, linguistics, and early American literature. Before teaching at IUP, Lea taught at Northeastern University, Babson College, and The University of Cincinnati. At IUP, Lea co-directed the Writing Center and was director of Liberal Studies English, as well as assistant chair of the English Department. She organized national, regional, and local conferences on writing centers at IUP and secured grants to support professional development workshops for faculty in writing pedagogy and practice across the curriculum. At IUP, she taught public speaking; support courses for underprepared students; college writing at all levels, including technical writing; a variety of literature courses; and an interdisciplinary senior seminar on national parks. She is the author of *Write at the Start: A Guide for Integrating Writing into Freshman Seminar Courses* (1993), monographs on writing centers, and numerous articles on teaching writing and preparing students to work as writing-center tutors. Her research and professional writing interests include a rhetorical approach to teaching style and voice, working with students with disabilities, and faculty-student collaboration.

**Tracy L. Skipper** is assistant director for publications for the National Resource Center for The First-Year Experience and Students in Transition at the University of South Carolina (USC). Before coming to the Center, she was director of residence life and judicial affairs at Shorter College in Rome, Georgia, where her duties included teaching in the college's first-year seminar program and serving as an academic advisor for first-year students. She also was director of student activities and residence life at Wesleyan College in Macon, Georgia. She edited (with Roxanne Argo) *Involvement in Campus Activities and the Retention of First-Year College Students* (2003), wrote *Student Development in the First College Year: A Primer for*

*College Educators* (2005), and contributed a chapter to *The Senior Year: Culminating Experiences and Transitions* (2012). She holds a bachelor's degree in psychology from USC, a master's degree in higher education from Florida State University, and a master's in American literature and doctorate in rhetoric and composition from USC. She has presented on the application of student development theory to curricular and cocurricular contexts and on the design and evaluation of writing assignments. Her research interests include the application of cognitive-structural development to composition pedagogy and the use of writing in first-year seminars. She teaches writing as an adjunct instructor in USC's English department.